Suber

A Literary Tour Guide
to England and Scotland

A Literary Tour Guide to England and Scotland

by Emilie C. Harting

WILLIAM MORROW AND COMPANY, INC.
New York   1976

Printed in the United States of America.

Library of Congress Cataloging in Publication Data

Harting, Emilie C
  A literary tour guide to England and Scotland.

  Includes index.
  1. Literary landmarks—Great Britain. 2. Great Britain—Description and
travel—1971-   —Guidebooks. I. Title.
PR109.H34 1976   914.1'04'857   75-22189
ISBN 0-688-02971-X

To Rob
for support,
patience,
and traveler's aid

Contents

Introduction

Since each county of Britain has a rich literary heritage, it would be infeasible for a guidebook to cover every site associated with an author. Thus two general criteria have been followed in selecting those sites to be included: (1) that they be associated with generally recognized authors; and (2) that they be either visible or open at least part of the year.

Travelers should find these hints helpful in their journeys to places described in this book:

(1) Use a comprehensive road map when touring the countryside and a thorough street map of London when in the city. While the maps in the book should be an aid in pointing out locations, reproducing areas in sufficient detail to include all minor roads is difficult.

(2) Ask directions whenever leaving a marked route Many places included are several miles from the nearest town. Another advantage of making queries can be discovering unusual spots along the way which would otherwise be overlooked.

(3) Use the index as a cross-reference to find places associated with authors and works.

(4) While every attempt has been made to include the most accurate and up-to-date data on open buildings, visitor's hours are always subject to change.

In the section on London many places associated with major authors have been grouped together into walks through different sections of the city. The accompanying index of authors and sites should be of help to the tourist searching for particular associations.

A Literary Tour Guide
to England and Scotland

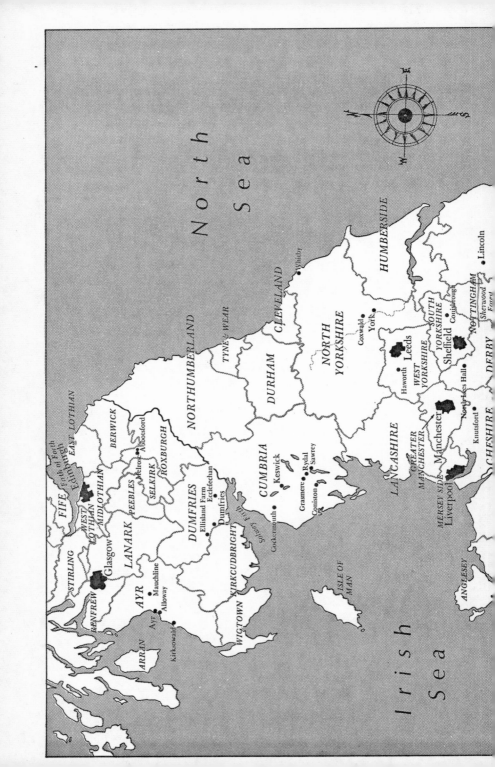

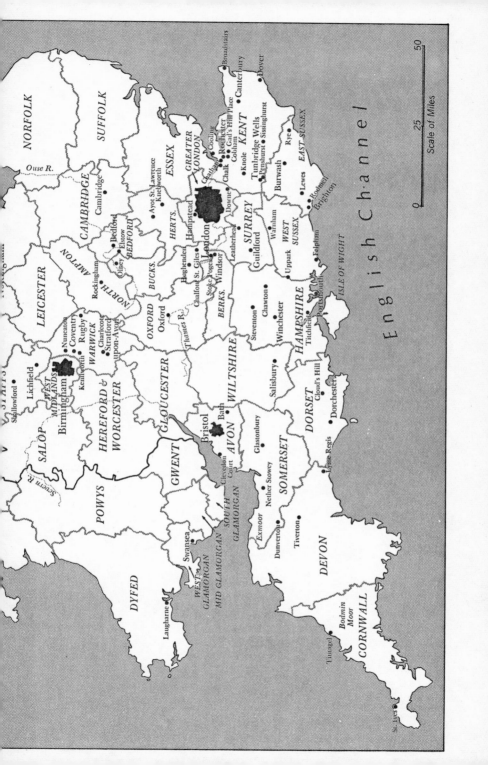

English and Scottish Towns
of Literary Interest
(listed alphabetically)

ABBOTSFORD (Roxburghshire): 3 mi. W of Melrose

In 1812 Sir Walter Scott brought his family, farmhands, domestic servants, and livestock to settle at the farm of Carlleyhole on the River Tweed. As the Waverley novels made him a literary success, he renamed the farm **Abbotsford** and started the ambitious building enlargements that made his estate one of the greatest in southern Scotland. Thus his boyhood dream of becoming a great border laird was fulfilled.

Abbotsford is a shrine to a writer who drew worldwide attention to Scotland in his many novels and poems, but also to a national hero in another sense. It was Scott who persuaded King George IV to open up a chest in the Crown Room of Edinburgh Castle and rediscover the Scottish regalia, which had been lost for over a hundred years. There had been no Scottish monarchs since 1603, and many Scotsmen suspected that the crown scepter and sword had been removed to England. As a result of Scott's perseverance, Edinburgh Castle now houses the Scottish regalia.

Scott's reverence for the past is seen throughout the house. In the elegant two-story library are the nine thousand volumes he accumulated, along with such items as Rob Roy's purse, Burns's tumbler with some of his verses scratched on it, and a lock of Prince Charles's hair. Many of the bindings are stamped in gilt with a portcullis and the words *"clausus tutus ero,"* approximately an anagram for "Gualterus Scotus." The collection, clearly well planned, illustrates the comfort Scott achieved a decade after arriving at the farmhouse. Prominently displayed are the two Scott family Bibles and other books of sentimental value to him. The richness of the room is especially seen in the oak paneling and shelves and in the intricately molded ceiling, copied from the Rosslyn Chapel.

Sir Walter's study, where he labored hard to pay off his debts by writing novels, is built in the same style as the library, with floor-to-ceiling shelves, and remains as he left it. In 1935 two secret drawers were discovered in his desk. One contained a sizeable number of the letters he and his wife exchanged before their marriage.

Of all the rooms, the North Armory most reflects the atmosphere of Scott's work. The walls are decorated heavily with his fine collection of arms. Among the hundreds of weapons are Sir Walter's blunderbuss, yeomanry sword, and pistol, Rob Roy's gun and broadsword, even James VI's hunting bottle. The South Armory, an equally impressive room, includes many paintings of family members, pets, and local scenes meaningful to Scott.

Scott memorabilia are spread around the entrance hall: the original keys of the prison of Midlothian, a glass case containing some of Sir Walter's clothes, and a bust of Wordsworth. But perhaps even more significant is the dining room where Scott died. Here you can stand in the window-alcove where Scott, after writing so gallantly to beat his impending bankruptcy, came to spend his last hours, overlooking the view of the Border Country and winding Tweed that he had celebrated so in his romantic novels.

(Abbotsford is open end Mar.–end Oct., Mon.–Sat. 10–5, Sun. 2–5. Small entry fee.)

ALLOWAY (Ayrshire): 2 mi. S of Ayr, on B7024

The low, whitewashed **Burns Cottage**, where Robert Burns spent his first seven years, is situated right on the main road in Alloway. Inside is the bed in which he was born, and some pieces of furniture thought to have been connected with the family. Two of the long rooms, the kitchen and parlor, were used as living quarters and the other two for horses, cows, and chickens. In fact, the feeding troughs are still on the walls.

Attached to the cottage is the **Burns Museum,** housing the most noteworthy Burns relics. These include the Burns family Bible, with entries in the poet's own hand, a perfect copy of the Kilmarnock edition of his works, along with many original manuscripts, letters, and poems. Copies of all the material are also photostated and kept in bindings for interested readers.

Only a few yards up the road is the entrance to the **Auld Kirkyard** (Old Churchyard), scene of the witches' orgy in "Tam O'Shanter." Tam supposedly started his late-evening ride at a pub on the site of the Tam O'Shanter Inn in the village of Kirksowald, several miles away, and ended up galloping through this churchyard, where he saw the witches dancing through the church windows, and on down a few hundred yards to the Brig o' doon, where he shook himself free of the witches after they had taken the tail of Maggie, his gray mare. Burns's father's tombstone is the first prominent gravestone inside the churchyard. A few yards behind it are the church ruins. Actually, most of the walls are still standing, so you can see the windows which Tam peeked through on that stormy evening.

A short distance down is the **Burns Monument,** a copy of the monument to Lysicrates in Athens. Within it are more relics of the poet—locks of his hair, his seal, and Highland Mary's Bibles. Farther down, on the other side of the road, is the Brig o' doon, the final scene in "Tam O'Shanter."

(Burns Cottage and Museum are open Apr.–Sept., weekdays 9–7, Sun. 2–7 except 10–7 in July and Aug. Oct., weekdays 9–6, Sun. 2–6. Nov.–Mar., weekdays 9–4. Nominal charge.)

AYOT ST. LAWRENCE   (Hertfordshire): 3 mi. NW of Welwyn, off A600

Shaw's Corner is not at the intersection of a cosmopolitan London suburb, as the address might imply. Rather it is a very secluded corner, reached by driving a series of long, meandering country lanes through the forests of Hertfordshire.

When Shaw came here to live permanently in 1906, *Arms and the Man, Caesar and Cleopatra, Man and Superman,* and *Candida* had already established him as a leading playwright in England and America. During his years at this house he continued with *Pygmalion, Saint Joan,* and a number of other great works. Active and creative until his last days, he lived at Shaw's Corner until 1950, when he died there at the age of ninety-four.

Though every cranny of the house reflects Shaw, the entrance hall in particular contains some interesting personal items. On the front door is an unusual brass knocker with the inscription "Man and Superman." Inside the front hall, above his glove box and sticks, is his famous collection of hats. One, a soft homburg, he wore for sixty years. Also near the door is the basket where he methodically sat to put on his shoes before going out. The Bechstein piano which meant so much to him is against the opposite wall. In 1888, under the pseudonym of Corno di Bassetto, he became the music critic of the *Star*. It is said that when the air-raid sirens wailed over Ayot a half-century later, Shaw often sat down at the piano and sang an Italian opera to his own accompaniment.

In the study, Shaw's main workroom, his large encumbered desk remains as he left it, scattered with the pens, gear, and pocket dictionaries he used for immediate reference. Around his desk hang photos of friends he especially admired, among them William Morris, whom Shaw described as "four great men rolled into one." The bookshelves around the side walls housed his compact working library, and the smaller desk to the left of his own was reserved for his secretary, Miss Patch. The meticulously organized collection of photographs housed in the filing cabinets next to his desk illustrates his competency as a photographer. For over fifty years, this was a favorite pastime, and he often carried his two cameras with him on trips to London and on walks in the area.

Near the couch, which he often used for resting, hangs an original cartoon by Bernard Partridge of Shaw rehearsing *Arms*

and the Man at the Avenue Theatre in 1894. There are also
some photographs with interesting associations, one in particular with Lord Howard de Walden, William Archer, James
Barrie, Chesterton, and Shaw, dressed as cowboys while acting
in a film by Barrie. It was drama critic William Archer, one of
Shaw's closest friends, who got him his first job as a journalist
in 1885.

The drawing room next to the study was Mrs. Shaw's room,
but aside from the portrait of her above the fireplace, there is
little evidence that she ever used it. Shaw's accolades are every-
where. On the chimneypiece is the Oscar awarded for *Pygmalion*
as the best film of 1938. In the bay window are three bronzes
by Prince Paul Troubetskoy, one representing Shaw in 1926,
and another of Rodin. On a small stool is the famous marble of
Shaw's hand by Sigmund Strobl, and at a large desk is the Rodin
bust which Shaw sat for at Meudon.

Shaw also used the dining room a great deal. He often read
with his lunch, sometimes spending as long as two hours at the
table. Then in the evening after an early dinner he would sit
in the armchair by the fire, again reading or listening to the
wireless until he went to bed. This room is filled with personal
relics, and the walls are lined with photographs illustrating his
early life in Dublin and the various personalities and causes he
identified with, among them Lenin, Stalin, Granville-Barker,
and Ibsen.

Through French doors in the dining room is the garden,
where he used to take a short walk each day before dinner. He
also did a lot of writing in the revolving summer house at the
bottom of the garden. There was complete quiet, safe from
the interruptions of friends and admirers. The wicker chair
in which he worked is still pulled up to the flap table, and one
of his favorite hats is up on the table among the pencils,
erasers and other writing tools.

(Shaw's Corner is open daily except Tues., 11–1 and 2–6; closed
mid-Dec.–mid-Jan., and Good Friday. Small entry fee.)

AYR   (Ayrshire): 33 mi. SW of Glasgow

Tam O'Shanter Museum: Famous the world over, this inn on a busy commercial street in Ayr is named after Robert Burns's drinking partner Douglas Graham, whom he nicknamed Tam O'Shanter. In a room just to the right of the front door is the original table Burns, Graham, and Souter Johnnie sat around while they quaffed the "reaming swats that drank divinely." Most of the walls of this tavern are covered with initials, more of them, it is hoped, from Burns's time than later. It also seems to be the repository for commemorative pieces given by Burns clubs around the world. There are over twenty-five pictures of the author in the five rooms open to the public. In addition to the many prints of Tam O'Shanter's ride are scenes from another famous poem, "The Cotter's Saturday Night." In display cases are many small personal possessions of the family, many those of the poet's wife, Jean Amour. Of special note is a cradle said to have been used by Burns.

(The museum is open weekdays in summer 9:30–5:30 and weekdays in winter 12–4; also Sun., June–Aug., 2–5:30. Nominal charge.)

BATH   (Avon): 13 mi. SE of Bristol

Known most for its Roman baths, this elegant city with its seemingly endless blocks of sand-colored Georgian houses has a long list of literary guests. Dramatist Richard Brinsley Sheridan wrote most of *The Rivals* while living on Terrace Walk in the 1770's, basing both that play and *The School for Scandal* on local scenes. A bit later, in the 1830's, Charles Dickens frequented the card room, now the Assembly Rooms of the **Museum of Costume,** and the city as a whole figures predominantly in several chapters of *Pickwick Papers*. The White Hart Inn of that novel is now the **Grand Pump Room Hotel,** and proprietor Moses Pickwick's grandfather clock is now on

display at the Dickens House on Doughty Street, London. It is
thought that he created the stories of *The Old Curiosity Shop*
and *Bleak House* here also, even though they are set elsewhere.

Jane Austen, who was here too during the early part of the
nineteenth century, is perhaps the writer who has said the
most for Bath. To her it provided the real experience of city
life—balls and card parties, theater and spas—since she visited
here much more frequently than London. It was not a place
she loved wholeheartedly, however. In her novel *Persuasion* she
gives a vivid picture of Bath in its heyday, and in *Northanger
Abbey* she provides us with a delicate satire on visitors to Bath.

Jane and her family often approached the city from the
London-to-Bath Road and came down over Kingdown Hill.
She frequently wrote about the silhouette of Lansdown Hill,
which runs steeply into the town with its Abbey Tower, church
spires, and chimney pots. The Austens stayed for the most part
at No. 1 the Paragon, conveniently located near the drinking
waters of the Pump Room and the dances and concerts at the
Assembly Rooms.

Those rooms, and in fact much of the city, came alive in the
two novels she set here. Catherine Morland, heroine of *Northanger Abbey*, was, like Jane Austen herself, a young girl when
taken by the Allens to reside in Bath for six weeks. Visiting the
Assembly Rooms soon after their arrival, they found themselves
ignored by the fashionable visitors until Catherine, clearly a
projection of Jane, met a suitable young gentleman and found
herself suddenly swept up in the cultural activities and shopping, which were unavailable at home. In keeping with romantic tradition, Catherine became engaged to Henry from
Northanger Abbey.

In *Persuasion* Jane Austen dealt with a later Bath, a period
some twenty years after *Northanger Abbey*. The characters were
older and Bath had begun to wane as a fashionable center. The
whole city seems more mellow in this novel, which is set in the
years following the Napoleonic Wars, when many retired
officers came to settle in the city. Jane was able to show her
distaste for the mixed crowds of the public halls and assemblies
by having the Elliots, her main characters, hold private parties
for select visitors. Apart from concerts at the Octagon Room

of the Upper Rooms, there are few references to public entertainments and not a word about dances. Instead of frequenting the Pump Room or the Crescent, her young character Anne met people frequently at small shops and restaurants.

Jane Austen exhibited her thorough knowledge of Bath and its surroundings by the extensive walks that her characters take. In *Northanger Abbey* Eleanor and Henry Tilney took the long walk to Beechen Cliff in the woodlands surrounding the city. She described "that noble hill whose beautiful verdure and hanging coppice render it so striking an object from almost every opening in Bath." Catherine also walked quite a bit around the steep hill of the city, often going back and forth between her own lodgings in Pulteney Street and those of her friends the Thorpes in the Edgar Buildings. Anne Elliott too walked up and down the steep hills from Camden Place, now Camden Crescent, to Westgate Buildings to visit Mrs. Smith. After calling on the Musgrove family near the Abbey she was able to make the journey on Captain Wentworth's arm and, "as they slowly pace the gradual ascent," was quite equal to indulging "in those explanations of what had directly preceded the present moment, which were so poignant and so ceaseless in interest." Touring the sites of Bath, the Assembly Rooms, and Pump House at the top of the hill, and the abbey down below, you appreciate the slow pace and deliberate contemplation of Jane Austen's characters.

Just outside Bath is **Prior Park,** the sham castle complete with Palladian bridge, built for Ralph Allen, who discovered the beauty of Bath stone and promoted the building of the Georgian city while reforming England's postal system. Henry Fielding is believed to have modeled Squire Allworthy of *Tom Jones* after Allen. The chapel and grounds are now a Catholic college. From the front steps of the central building is a breathtaking view over the Palladian bridge to Bath.

(The Assembly Rooms are open all year except Dec. 25, weekdays in summer 9:30–6, in winter 10–5; Sun. in summer 11–6, in winter 10–5. Small entry fee. Prior Park chapel and grounds are open all year, daily except Sun., 11–4; the mansion is open May–Sept., on Tues. and Wed., and in Aug. Mon.–Thurs., 2–6. Small entry fee.)

BEDFORD   (Bedfordshire): 50 mi. N of London

In 1660, when the restoration of the monarchy brought the
Puritan regime of Cromwell to an end, Baptist preacher and
later-to-be-famous author John Bunyan was charged as "a common upholder of unlawful meetings." For the next twelve years
Bunyan suffered imprisonment in Bedford's Old County Jail,
since he refused to promise that he would cease holding Baptist
congregations. It was during his long stay here that he wrote
Pilgrim's Progress as well as many other works.

There are numerous reminders of Bunyan around the town.
His bronze **statue** by Sir Joseph Boehm stands at the northern
end of High Street, close to the Saxon tower of the Church of
St. Peter de Merton. Its pedestal is decorated with bas-relief
scenes from *Pilgrim's Progress*. Also, **commemorative stones**
mark the site of the two jails where he was imprisoned: the Old
County Jail, which formerly stood at the junction of High
Street and Silver Street, and the Town Jail, which was on the
old bridge over the River Ouse.

The **Bunyan Meeting** is on Mill Street, on the site of a barn
used as a church upon his release from prison in 1672. Its doors,
which took ten years to complete, contain ten bronze panels,
each depicting a scene from the famous book. A prison door
from the Old County Jail is preserved in the vestibule. In the
same building is a museum containing the most complete collection of Bunyan relics in existence. The walls are lined with
pictures of him in jail and various illustrations from *Pilgrim's
Progress*. Bookshelves are filled with copies of his works in many
languages. And there's a piece of his gravestone from Bunhill
Fields cemetery in London, as well as the pulpit from which
he preached until convicted. Display cases contain relics such
as the flute he made from the rails of a stool while he was in
prison, his portable anvil, marquetry cabinet, beer tankard,
and his deed of gift (will), along with a number of examples
of his handwriting. Also, the **Bedford Public Library** on Harpur
Street has a noted collection of over eight hundred editions of
Bunyan's works and related studies.

In 1653 Bunyan joined the congregation of Bedford's **St. John's Church,** whose pastor was the dissenter John Gifford. The old rectory, which still stands beside the church, was undoubtedly the building he had in mind as the House of the Interpreter in *Pilgrim's Progress,* since Gifford was the original of the interpreter. After attending here for a while Bunyan followed in Gifford's footsteps by going out to preach in the neighboring villages.

In Bunyan's day sanitation was practically nonexistent, even in a town as important as Bedford. An open gulley, running down the middle of the street, was a common receptacle for refuse of all kinds. As the unsavory odors reached Bunyan through his jail window, he dreamed of the fresh air of the fields and the country roads he knew so well, and wrote of the Valley of the Shadow of Death "full of great stinks and loathsome smells."

(Bunyan Meeting is open all year, Tues.–Fri., 10–12 and 2–4:30. Nominal charge.)

BODMIN MOOR   (Cornwall): 25 mi. W of Plymouth

Probably the most famous literary pilgrimage in Cornwall is to **Jamaica Inn,** the gaunt gray-stone inn on the lonely road across Bodmin Moor, which Daphne du Maurier has immortalized in her novel of the same name. Just as in the book, the place is charged with atmosphere. Also nearby is **Frenchman's Creek,** a hidden inlet of the Helford River, where she set another historical romance. The actual creek lies about half a mile west of Helford village, on the river's south bank.

BRIGHTON   (Sussex)

In his long narrative poem *Don Juan,* Byron wrote "Shut up—not the King, but the Pavilion/Or else 'twill cost us another million." The **Royal Pavilion** is still Brighton's chief tourist attraction. Byron was invited to the Prince's birthday celebration here in 1808, perhaps because the latter was intrigued by the many rumors of the poet's romantic exploits and wild lifestyle. At the time the Prince himself was resented for the manner in which he poured large sums from the country's treasury into the garish palace, where his mistresses resided with him.

During the early part of the nineteenth century **Brighton Camp** was the most popular military post on the southern coast. The officers often gave military parades and reviews, and Brighton became a mecca for young girls who fancied themselves walking along the Promenade on the arm of a handsome young officer. Lydia, in Jane Austen's *Pride and Prejudice,* had fantasies of visiting the camp, a mirage of tents crowded with festive young people, and at one point imagined herself flirting with six officers at a time.

Thackeray spent much time here in the 1840's and stayed at the **Old Ship Hotel** in the town center while writing *Vanity Fair,* which has a number of settings in the town. George and Amelia spent their honeymoon here, and several of the officers waited in Brighton to be called over to the Continent in the battle against Napoleon. Lord Steyne is thought to have been modeled in part after the Prince of Wales's friend Lord Hertford, and the salvationist Lady Southdown after the mother of Lord Huntington, who founded a Nonconformist church in North Street. Thackeray wrote many articles on Brighton for *Punch,* and at one point described it as gay and gaudy, like a harlequin's jacket. Both Thackeray and Dickens were guests at literary parties held in the private salon of novelist Horace Smith at 21 **Sillwood Place,** and they both gave lectures at the Town Hall. Dickens stayed at the **Bedford Hotel** while writing most of *Bleak House* and *Dombey and Son,* and, in fact, made the elder Mr. Dombey a guest there in the novel.

Arnold Bennett gave a graphic description of Brighton during the late Victorian era in his novel *Hilda Lessways.* The characters from the *The Old Wives' Tale* and other novels of the Five Towns viewed Brighton as a town of wealth and luxury which contrasted strongly with such northern "pleasure cities" as Blackpool and Llandudno.

During the 1940's Brighton residents were incensed by Graham Greene's novel *Brighton Rock* and the film based upon it, since they thought it portrayed the town as a gangster-ridden resort. Actually what the sensational press played up in its reviews of the book was not the mainstream of the resort but the racecourse, public houses, dance halls, and amusement arcades in a very restricted quarter of the town.

(The Royal Pavilion is open daily Oct.–June 10–5 and July–Sept. 10–8. Closed Dec. 25, Boxing Day, and 3 days at end of June. Small entry fee.)

BROADSTAIRS   (Kent): 4 mi. SE of Margate

During Dickens' time the dark, fortresslike mansion up on the cliffs above the seaside resort of Broadstairs was called Fort House. Since then the name has been changed to **Bleak House** and an entire west wing has been added, but the whole of the house that Dickens occupied still stands; visitors can enter the little study in which he worked, the large bedroom in which he slept, and the dining room in which he and his friends feasted in the hearty manner characteristic of the Victorian age. Though Dickens sometimes stayed at a hotel or one of the smaller houses away from the seafront, this was "the residence most desired" while in Broadstairs. He lived in it throughout summer and autumn for many years.

The actual Bleak House of the novel by that name is vaguely described as being on the top of a hill in the open country somewhere near St. Albans. However, this house, because of its gloomy appearance and awesome position, was an inspiration for *Bleak House*. In fact, Dickens spent several months planning the book's broad outline in his study here. That room, in which he also wrote the whole of *David Copperfield,* has become the focal point of the house.

It is hardly a writer's dark little alcove set off from the rest of the house. His desk stands in front of a window with a clear, uninterrupted view straight out across the North Sea. On one wall of the spacious room is a reproduction of the

famous "The Empty Chair" by Sir Luke Fildes. This picture
shows Dickens' more elaborate study, the day after his death,
at Gad's Hill Place, the stately mansion which was his last
residence. That mansion, Cobham Hall, is now a girls' school,
and the study is open only occasionally by appointment.

Along the walls are several displays devoted to works closely
connected with the house. One showcase devoted to *David
Copperfield* contains one of the finest sets of the original
monthly parts, a copy of the first bound edition, and a pocket
edition once carried around by Prime Minister Ramsay Mac-
Donald. Another case contains a fine set of the original monthly
shilling parts of *Bleak House*. In addition to a number of interesting photographs, letters, and manuscripts is an early photo-
graph of the author's young actress friend, Miss Ellen Tiernan.

Bleak House has been restored to reflect the lifestyle of the
Dickens family there. The billiard room contains many personal belongings in addition to family letters and photographs.
Dickens, who loved billiards and cards, probably spent considerable time here with his children. On the walls of the main
corridor is a small collection of rare theatrical posters of plays
based on his novels. His bedroom contains a large brass bed
he may have slept in at the Bull Hotel in Rochester. The dining
room, in which he described himself as often "eating a strong
lunch after walking a dozen miles or so," has been decorated
with period furniture.

(Bleak House is open Easter–Oct., daily 2–5, and an hour later in
July–Aug. Nominal charge.)

Dickens Museum: This house on the seafront was occupied
by formidable spinster Mary Pearson Strong, so proud of the
strip of lawn in front of her house that when donkeys tres-
passed on it she would chase them and their riders with a
broom. The young Dickens, a regular visitor to the house, used
to chuckle at the lady's eccentricities. Sometime later his pen
moved the setting to Dover and Miss Strong became the no-less-
formidable Betsey Trotwood, who did her donkey chasing on
the pages of *David Copperfield*.

The museum houses largely a collection of prints and illustrations related to that novel and "Our Watering Place," a

famous article in which Dickens showed deep affection for this seaside town. The room he used as a model for Betsey Trotwood's parlor has been furnished according to David Copperfield's description and a sketch by the book's illustrator, Phiz. Here is the cupboard from which Betsey Trotwood gathered the ingredients for the alarming concoction she administered to the fainting David, as well as a mahogany sideboard which belonged to Dickens himself. On the second floor are many copies of the illustrations for "Our Watering Place" and a number of eighteenth- and nineteenth-century prints of Broadstairs.

(Dickens Museum is open Apr.–Oct., daily 2:30–5:30; mid-May–mid-Sept. it is also open Tues., Wed., Thurs. evenings 7–9.)

BURWASH   (East Sussex): 13 mi. S of Tunbridge Wells

Bateman's, the home where Rudyard Kipling came to settle for the last half of his life, is tucked away in the rolling hills of the Sussex countryside. When he came here at age thirty-six, he was already a renowned writer. In fact, he had become so sought after that he had searched for a place like Bateman's to protect himself from publicity seekers. The house, a fine example of Jacobean country architecture, had been built by the owner of nearby Nether Forge in 1634, when ironmaking was the chief industry in Sussex. Kipling restored the house to his own tastes, keeping its seventeenth-century character, and furnishing it with family pieces from India and the Orient. He also got the mill working again, thanks to a friend who had worked on the Assuan Dam, and after laying a cable from the mill to the house, was one of the first in Sussex to have electricity.

Though he became immersed in the Sussex landscape, the management of Bateman's was left to his wife. He was above all a persevering craftsman, who spent many hours each day writing and rewriting his manuscripts. During his first decade here he produced three significant works: *Traffics and Discoveries, Puck of Pook's Hill*—the hill is visible from the back of the house looking west—and *Rewards and Fairies*. The last two volumes, which Kipling said had to be read by children before people realized that they were meant for grown-ups, contained stories which Kipling thought were the best he'd ever written. He often acted out these stories with his children and their friends under the trees surrounding the house, and at times used the grazing donkeys and cows as characters.

Those three works marked the end of the "Kipling of the East," and his emergence as a writer drawing on the history and feeling of the Kent and Sussex countryside. *If* and *The Glory of the Garden* were also written here, and quite near the end of his life he began his autobiographical work, *Something of Myself*, in part a memorial to Bateman's.

Kipling's study remains exactly as he left it. Along two walls is his library, heavily stacked with naval histories, travel books from India and Africa, folklore, and a number of his favorite authors, among them Defoe, Carlyle, Thackeray, Stevenson, and Pepys. Of special interest is the eighteenth-century chair, whose club feet have been fitted with blocks so that it is exactly the height for his ten-foot-long Jacobean table. Many of the objects on the table were described by Kipling when he spoke of his "working tools"—his piles of off-white paper, his canoe-shaped pen tray holding used brushes and pens, and the inkwell on which he etched the title of every book he had published.

A large room next to the study, originally a guest room, is now an exhibition area containing a powder closet and a statue of a seventeenth-century Sussex iron founder standing proudly among his wares. The eight plaques on the wall there are illustrations for *Kim, Soldiers Three,* and several short stories, all done by the author's father, John Lockwood Kipling.

A visit to Bateman's is not complete without a stroll through the grounds at the back of the house. Just beyond the south terrace is the pond Kipling built so his children could bathe and sail their small boats. Then through the garden gate the path leads to a natural garden with many flowering shrubs and trees, and, farther on, to the Dudwell trout stream and the old water mill.

(Bateman's is open Mar.–Oct. daily except Fri. 2–6, plus 11–12:30 June–end Sept. Small entry fee.)

CAMBRIDGE   (Cambridgeshire): 50 mi. N of London

Cambridge University: Literary associations abound in this university city. Many of the pioneers of English literature, among them Milton, Spenser, and Ben Jonson, were trained at the beautiful colleges here on the River Cam. The more modern Wordsworth wrote almost all of his great poetry as a young revolutionary Cambridge graduate of St. John's, and Byron's memorial to his dog—Boatswain's monument, at Newstead Abbey—is the result of a whim he had while at Trinity College. His alma mater's library has the statue of Byron that was absolutely refused by the authorities at Westminster Abbey.

Almost the first sight in Cambridge is cathedral-like **King's College Chapel,** whose beautiful pinnacles are visible long before you reach the city center. The chapel itself dominates the King's Parade. Inside, twenty-four magnificent sixteenth-century stained-glass windows stretch in tiers almost from the floor to the ceiling. When sunshine streams through the windows, shafts of many colors dance about the room, and as the organ fills the chapel with music you realize how the grandeur of the building inspired the sonnets of William Wordsworth.

Across the quadrangle is an open archway which leads to the River Cam and the smooth, sloping lawns of **the Backs,** so called because the rear elevation of several of the colleges face the river. With their tree-lined riverside walks, the Backs form one of the great attractions of Cambridge. Here are some beautiful views of the colleges from the river. One of the best is from the Bridge of Sighs, linking the two courts of St. John's College. At this point the water laps the walls of the college library, whose displays include some early examples of William Caxton's printing.

Through a castellated gateway is the spacious Great Court of **Trinity College** with its canopied fountain. Among its famous scholars are Tennyson, Bacon, and Wordsworth. Across the river and set a little apart from the other colleges is Magdalene, whose library contains books and manuscripts given by the diarist Samuel Pepys on his death in 1703. The collection includes the original six-volume manuscript of the famous diary, laid open so that visitors can see the shorthand that so long baffled decipherers.

Farther on, past King's College, are **Corpus Christi** and **St. Catherine's,** facing each other close to the junction of King's Parade and Trumpington Street. On the fourteenth-century Old Court at Corpus Christi is a plaque indicating the windows of the room where the Elizabethan playwright Christopher Marlowe lived when he was an undergraduate here.

(Colleges are open to the public most days during daylight hours.)

CANTERBURY   (Kent): 50 mi. E of London

Modern pilgrims to Canterbury enter the city by the same **West Gate** that Chaucer and his entourage used over eight hundred years ago when they came here from London to pay respects to Archbishop Thomas à Becket, who was murdered in the **Cathedral** by four knights in 1170, the year the building was completed.

Though almost nothing in the Cathedral is now arranged as it was in the twelfth century, Becket's footsteps can be traced along the arcaded wall of the cloisters and into the Cathedral through the northwest door. Legend has it that the monks with him barred the door, knowing that the knights were coming, but Becket insisted the bars be removed. Soon the knights burst in, an argument ensued, and Becket threw one man to the floor. But the others drew their swords and Becket was dead after three slashes. A simple memorial sculpture has been placed on the wall just above the spot where he is said to have fallen. You can envision him coming through the doorway just to the right as he did immediately before his death in 1170, and more recently during the premiere performance of T. S. Eliot's *Murder in the Cathedral.*

Becket's body was first buried in the Cathedral crypt and later moved to an elaborate shrine behind Trinity Chapel. It is said that the shrine encasing the tomb was covered with great plates of gold encrusted with diamonds, rubies, emeralds, and other jewels. For three centuries, countless pilgrims came to venerate St. Thomas and to seek the miraculous cures which purportedly occurred at the site. Some of them are pictured in the beautiful, glowing, stained-glass "miracle windows" encircling the shrine area. In 1538, however, King Henry VIII ordered the shrine destroyed, Becket's bones scattered, and all trace of the saint erased. By this act Henry was said to have enriched his own treasury with twenty-six cartloads of gold and jewels.

Charles Dickens was a frequent visitor to Canterbury, especially during the last years of his life, when he lived at nearby Gad's Hill. Much of *David Copperfield* is set here, and the core of this picturesque city has changed little since that time. In the novel he describes how the old houses and gateways and "the still nooks, where the ivied growth of centuries crept over gabled ends and ruined walls" had a softening effect on his spirit. Dickens often stayed at the **Fountains Hotel** in St. Margaret's Street, the County Inn where Mr. Dick slept when visiting David Copperfield. The "little inn" where Mr. Micawber stayed is thought to be the **Sun Hotel** in Sun Street. Dr. Strong's School, where David was sent by his aunt, is, of course, the **King's School** within the Cathedral grounds. Dr. Strong's residence was probably the corner building, No. 1, on **Lady Wootton's Green,** while the charming old house at **71 St. Dunstan's Street** is thought to have been Mr. Wickfield's residence. Among great writers who attended here were Christopher Marlowe and Somerset Maugham. In fact, this is the school in Maugham's *Of Human Bondage.*

CHALFONT ST. GILES (Buckinghamshire): on A413, 2 mi. N of A40

In July, 1665, while plague was raging through London, the blind poet Milton, his wife, and daughter left their home in the Bunhill Fields section to retreat to the remote village of Chalfont, where his former Latin pupil and reader Thomas Ellwood, later imprisoned as a practicing Quaker, had found him a "Pretty Box." This is the little red-brick house now referred to as **Milton's Cottage.**

During his short time there he was able to complete a long-delayed work. He had laid aside *Paradise Lost* twenty years earlier to throw all his energies into the Parliamentary cause. Then in 1660 came the Restoration. All the work he had done for the Commonwealth was gone; two of his books, *Eikono-clastes* and the *Defense of the English People,* were ordered to be called in and burned by the common hangman; and for a while he was forced to hide.

The simple cottage on a remote lane was no doubt a retreat for the then blind, disappointed poet. Since he no longer had any active part in the country's political movements, he was able to set himself back twenty years and devote all his energies to finishing *Paradise Lost.* Soon after his return to London he began work on *Paradise Regained.* Thomas Ellwood, who gave him constant encouragement on the two epic poems, and, in fact, suggested that he write a sequel to *Paradise Lost,* is buried only two miles away.

The two-room cottage, built near the end of the sixteenth century, had a succession of owners until the Milton Cottage Trust was formed in 1887. The kitchen houses relics common in Buckingham during the seventeenth century. On display is a valuable collection of various tools for lacemaking, then the chief occupation of the county's women, and, in addition, pictures of Chalfont from Milton's time to the present.

The second room was Milton's study, where he sat by the fireplace for long periods of time, dictating *Paradise Lost* to his wife and daughter. Above the mantel is the agreement of sale for that work, which made Milton and, in turn, the cottage famous. It went for a mere ten pounds. The study now has become a library lined with first editions of Milton's works in many languages. There are even copies of *Comus* in Japanese and *Paradise Regained* in Portuguese. Also represented on the shelves are Milton's Quaker contemporaries in the neighborhood, William Penn and Thomas Ellwood, who, along with many others of their persuasion, were imprisoned for their beliefs during the time he was here at the cottage.

As almost any writer's memorial, the cottage displays a piece of Milton's hair and a few small objects thought to have been his. Among the portraits and busts displayed around the cottage are Van der Gucht's copy of what is known as the Onslow portrait, and several etchings by Cipriani of this and other portraits. For those interested in the Commonwealth cause, of which Milton was so much a part, there are cannonballs believed to have been fired by Cromwell's soldiers when they camped in the Silsden meadow. The balls were found embedded in the roof of the local church.

(Milton's Cottage is open Feb.–Oct. weekdays except Tues. 10–1, 2:15–6 and Sun. 2:15–6; Nov.–Jan. only Sat. 10–1, Sun. 2:15–6. Nominal charge.)

CHALK   (Kent): off A227, N of Gravesend

In this picturesque village near Rochester, a plaque marks the house where Dickens spent his honeymoon and began *Pickwick Papers*. Over the entrance to **Chalk Church** is the quaint stone figure of an old priest, stooping, with an upturned vessel. Dickens is said to have greatly admired this stone figure, and to have taken his hat off to it whenever he passed by.

CHARLECOTE   (Warwickshire): 5 mi. NE of Stratford-upon-Avon

Shakespeare's connections here have been stressed since 1769, when David Garrick organized his great Shakespeare festival at Stratford-upon-Avon. Since then a visit to Stratford and "Shakespeare Country" has not been thought complete without a stop at the idyllic country estate **Charlecote Park.** The great house, almost a half-mile from the entrance at the end of a tree-lined path, faces on the Avon River. All through the tranquil grounds deer and Spanish sheep graze under large trees.

Since the twelfth century this has been the home of the Lucy family, and it is in the great hall that William Shakespeare was supposedly brought to trial before Sir Thomas Lucy, then the resident magistrate, for poaching on the grounds. Legend has it that this was a dramatic event in the poet's life and that he was probably fined, possibly flogged, and perhaps threatened with prison. Shakespeare was supposed to have retaliated by writing ribald verses about Sir Thomas and sticking them to the gatehouse. After he found himself a sought-after local troublemaker he was more or less forced to flee to London, where he established his lasting fame.

A bit later Shakespeare brought Sir Thomas onstage as a figure of fun, first in *Henry IV, Part II,* and then in *The Merry Wives of Windsor.* It is very easy to see the parallel between Justice Swallow and Sir Thomas. The reference to the "dozen white luces" in Swallow's coat of arms makes the connection quite convincing, since the arms of the Lucys are a series of pikes rising into the air. Also, Swallow complained to Falstaff that the latter had killed his deer and broken open his lodge. Shakespeare poked fun at Justice Swallow's special foible, his pride over his "old coat" of arms and long descent. This corresponds exactly with what is known of Sir Thomas Lucy's pride in his family's shield. Whenever it was mentioned he was said to have replied that it was "a very old coat too." Midway through the play Falstaff planned to get hold of some of Swallow's money, "as surely as the large pike makes a meal of freshwater fish," and referred to him contemptuously as "the old pike." Also Swallow appeared on the Commission of Array. Sir Thomas sat on just such a commission in 1565.

Falstaff once remarked to Swallow that he had "a goodly dwelling and rich." That same observation was made by Sir Walter Scott and Henry James as they were expressing thanks for the hospitality of the Lucys. Letters describing their visits are on display on the second floor of the house.

(Charlecote Park is open Apr. and Oct., Sat. and Sun. 11–5; Easter Week and May–Sept., daily except Mon. 11–5. Admission charged.)

CHATHAM (Kent): on A2, just over the city line from Rochester

Chatham is another Dickens area. It appears interchangeably with Rochester as Dudborough in *The Uncommercial Traveller* and Mudfog in *Mudfog Papers*. Dickens came to Chatham in 1816 and lived here from the age of four until the age of nine while his father was an officer in the Navy Pay Office. His favorite childhood home still stands at **11 Ordinance Terrace** and, as of this writing, there is a movement to save the house; his boyhood experiences and the friends and neighbors he knew here are vividly described in *Pickwick Papers* and *Sketches by Boz*. Another house, at **2 Ordinance Terrace,** where he also lived as a boy, had a great influence on *David Copperfield*. **Chatham's dockyard** is also thought to be the dockyard of *A Tale of Two Cities*.

CHAWTON (Hampshire): 1 mi. SW of Alton on A31 bypass

Chawton House, where Jane Austen lived with her widowed mother and sister Cassandra for the last eight years of her life, is a literary house revealing much of the author's world. Though only a few pieces of family furniture remain, each room is decorated in eighteenth-century style and contains many letters, illustrations, and descriptive material related to her life and works.

The dining room, with its polished wood and delicate wallpaper, is a scene cut out of a middle-class Austen novel. Here Jane closed all the doors and wrote her six great works while sitting at the table. She never allowed the creaking door which led from this room to the front to be fixed. During most of her time at Chawton she kept her authorship secret from all but close family—and the sound was her warning that a servant, visitor, or neighborhood child was coming and she had better hide her manuscript. The walls are now hung with series of letters written by her father, mother, and sister to various friends and acquaintances; and among them are several describing the events leading up to Jane's death. The correspondence between Mrs. Austen and her sister-in-law, in which she talks of her distaste for London, is especially interesting in light of the Austens' long association with the smaller but nevertheless cosmopolitan city of Bath.

Jane also spent considerable time in the dining room, which contains the original Austen furniture, her own worktable, and a clavichord similar to the one she played in this room. On it are her original music books. The adjoining vestibule contains a number of exhibits, including a facsimile portrait of Jane taken from the original of the drawing by her sister now in the National Gallery. Here also are photostatic copies of Jane's most interesting letters, many of them bearing important references to her novels.

Each upstairs room deserves careful perusal. There are innumerable prints, letters, and articles pertinent to her work, in addition to a number of personal relics revealing the domestic side of her personality. Her sister Cassandra wrote that Jane was quite adept at the fashionable overcast and satin stitch so popular in her day, and that handiness and neatness were among her characteristics. Jane's skill is displayed in the beautiful patchwork quilt and other handiwork in the glass cases. On the walls are sister Cassandra's pencil sketchings and original illustrations by Ellen Hill for the well-known work titled *Jane Austen, her Homes and Friends.* Particularly important are photostatic copies of the verses Jane wrote several days before her death; Sir Walter Scott's diary entry recording his appreciation of her writing, especially *Pride and Prejudice;* and the autographed remarks by Winston Churchill in a quotation from his great work *The Second World War.*

On the walls of the upstairs corridor hang printer's proofs of illustrations for *Pride and Prejudice* and photostatic copies of letters Jane wrote to her brothers. The other rooms contain clothes and childhood memorabilia of Jane and her siblings. One in particular has photographs of writing she did as a young girl.

Outside, to the rear of the house, is a shed, the former wash-house; this contains the donkey cart Jane used to ride around the countryside and the baking tools she used to place loaves and cakes in the oven of the old baking house. Baking was, at times, a favorite chore of hers.

(Chawton House is open Apr.–Oct., daily 11–4:30; Nov.–Mar., Wed.–Sun. 11–4:30. Nominal charge.)

While Jane, her sister, and mother lived at this house, her brother Edward lived a half-mile away at **Chawton Great House,** which he had inherited from his benefactor. Here, and at Edward's previous estate, Godmersham Park in eastern Kent, Jane got material for such upper-class novels as *Emma* and *Mansfield Park*. She came here often, both as a member of the family and as a guest at social affairs. She was clearly the poor relative Fanny Price of Mansfield Park, visiting her brother and sister-in-law Sir and Lady Bertram, and was as much aware of the goings-on of the estate as she was of her own middle-class dwelling down the road. The grounds can be reached by taking the second turn to the left on the road to Foreham. The view of the magnificent house and rolling lawn is a page out of *Emma*. Near the main road is the little chapel of St. Nicholas, at one time part of the estate. Jane's mother and sister Cassandra are buried in the churchyard there. (Jane is buried at Winchester Cathedral.)

CLEVEDON COURT (Avon): 14 mi. W of Bristol

Though **Clevedon Court**'s literary associations are largely nineteenth century, the fourteenth-century manor house is one of the few complete houses of that time which has survived. It stands at the foot of a line of hills stretching some ten miles east to Leigh Down and Avon Grange, and as other great houses of its period, has a Great Hall with stone floors, an arched chapel, State bedrooms, and walls lined with great works of art.

Clevedon's noted literary visitor was William Makepeace Thackeray, a frequent guest who sketched and wrote in what

once had been the chapel and was then the boudoir of the
State Bedroom. His Clevedon drawings were reproduced in a
brochure, "William Makepeace Thackeray at Clevedon Court,"
and two of his original drawings are still in the house. *Henry
Esmond* was partly drafted at Clevedon; and Lady Castlewood,
as well as many of Thackeray's other female characters, is based
on Jane Octavia—daughter of Sir Charles Elton, Master of
Clevedon, and wife of Rev. Henry Brookfield—with whom
Thackeray fell in love after his young wife, Isabella, became
insane. You can easily visualize many Thackeray scenes and
personages in this great house and its surroundings.

Sir Charles was also the uncle of Arthur Hallam of Tennyson's *In Memoriam*. When Hallam died in Vienna in 1833 his
body was brought back to Clevedon and buried in the Elton
Vault at nearby St. Andrew's. Tennyson stayed at Clevedon
Court when he visited Hallam's tomb in 1850, the year *In
Memoriam* was published. He wrote that it was "a kind of
consecration" to go there and visit the memorial at "this obscure and solitary church."

Many areas of the house contain objects associated with the
authors who have stayed here. At the top of the Georgian staircase near the Great Hall hangs Sir Joseph Edgar Boehm's
remarkable full-length cartoon of Thackeray—legs set firmly
apart, hands in trouser pockets, frock coat thrown back, chin
jutting forward under a head of white hair. It is a study for a
bronze statuette, one copy of which is in the National Portrait
Gallery. Beyond him the passage leads through the so-called
Thackeray Room, where there are portraits of Thackeray, Jane
Octavia Brookfield, and the Hallam family.

In the State Room, or Solar, is the famous "Travelers' Breakfast" by Edward Villiers Rippingille. It portrays many of the
contributors to *The London Magazine* and a number of Elton
family members. Charles Lamb is handing Rippingille the bill.
Coleridge is holding out a boiled egg for Wordsworth to sniff,
while Dorothy Wordsworth, in a black bonnet, sits at the table
with folded hands. Meanwhile Robert Southey ogles Julia
Elizabeth, Charles Abraham's daughter, pouring tea, while her
father looks out, grinning. In another painting, "Canynge's

Funeral," an allegory of Bristol civic life, poet Thomas Chatterton appears holding a lute, and one of the background figures is Robert Southey.

(Clevedon Court is open Apr.–end Sept., Wed., Thurs., Sun. 2:30–5:30. Small entry fee.)

CLOUD'S HILL   (Dorset): 8 mi. NW of Wareham, off A3390

Cloud's Hill: This cottage surrounded by rhododendron and sheltering pines is a good example of a writer's simple retreat. T. E. Lawrence rented it in 1923, when as a private in the Tank Corps he was stationed at nearby Bovington Camp. After repairing the structure to its present form he settled in, using it as a place of refuge whenever he could escape from duty. He would come here late in the day to work on *Seven Pillars of Wisdom* as he sat by the fire and played Beethoven and Mozart on the Gramophone.

Novelist E. M. Forster often visited then, and spoke of the brownish sitting room, with its wooden beams and ceiling, where guests from Bovington Camp talked, played Beethoven symphonies, and drank. Many of Lawrence's friends visited regularly and the cottage was the scene of suppers cooked by T. E., followed by heated discussions which went on way into the morning.

After the proceeds from his translation of *The Odyssey* enabled him to make an extensive series of improvements, Cloud's Hill became a retirement cottage. In 1935, after a few months of peace, which he described to friends as an era of "earthly paradise," Lawrence had a fatal crash on his motorcycle while going from the cottage to Bovington Camp. The property is now a National Trust.

(Cloud's Hill is open Apr.–end Sept., 2–6 daily; Oct.–end Mar. 12–4 daily. Small entry fee.)

COBHAM   (Kent): 5 mi. W of Rochester

Five miles from Rochester is the **Leather Bottle** at Cobham, where the lovesick Tracy Tupman of *Pickwick Papers* sought asylum. Inside the inn is a Pickwick Room full of Dickensian furniture and pictures.

COCKERMOUTH   (Cumbria): 8 mi. E of Workington on A594

Few writers have spoken so profoundly of their childhood as William Wordsworth. In his great autobiographical poem, *The Prelude,* in which he so clearly perceived the child as "father of the man," he saw "in simple childhood something of the base on which thy greatness stands." It was here at **Wordsworth House,** and in the surrounding woods and fields, that the "fair seed time" of his life was spent.

Almost from birth Wordsworth learned to commune with nature. He wrote that the River Derwent "blended with his nurse's song," and was a playmate which he and his siblings dearly loved. The sandy fields he ran through after spending the summer's day bathing in the river are those across the river from the house. Nearby were the ruins of the castle, through whose "green courts" he loved to chase the butterflies, pretending they were Frenchmen, and climb the castle turrets, plucking the golden flowers that grew in the crannies of the stones. To Cockermouth Castle he attributed his spirit of adventure and said that while wandering around its grounds he felt his first sense of the mysterious and incomprehensible. Perhaps the dungeon with its "soul-appalling darkness" gave him early introduction to thoughts of death. Eight miles away was the beach at Whitehaven, whose white water breaking against the quays and piers made a lasting impression upon him also. He wrote about the "mysterious awe with which he used to listen to anything said about storms and shipwrecks."

Wordsworth lost his parents at an early age, his father when he was thirteen and his mother when he was eight. Later in life he always looked back to his years at his childhood home in Cockermouth as a time when his character was formed by a happy and secure family unit, guided by parents who encouraged their children in a healthy outdoor life. The Wordsworths spent much time reading together. The poet's father fed the children with old-time stories of romance which triggered their imagination and kept them alive with a sense of wonder and mystery—*Don Quixote, Gulliver's Travels,* and Fielding's novels—rather than the moral tales for children which were flooding the market at that time. Cockermouth also remained dear to Wordsworth since it was where his great love of Dorothy, his sister, began. Their favorite playground was the hedge at the foot of the now overgrown garden. It is possible to walk there today and envision the place where one of the most celebrated relationships in literary history began.

Wordsworth House, an austere north-country version of a typical mid-Georgian house, looks much the same as it must have during the time the Wordsworths lived here. Except for a few dishes and a bookcase, none of the Wordsworth furniture remains. The house has been hung with portraits to reveal the literary scene of the Lake District during the poet's time. Wordsworth was a literary magnet and many of the foremost writers of the day came to visit him in the Lakes, at Dove Cottage in Grasmere, and at Rydal Mount, and some of them settled in the area.

Among the friends and contemporaries whose portraits hang in the dining room are Coleridge, with whom he collaborated on *Lyrical Ballads;* Sir Walter Scott, whose novels he enjoyed so; Robert Southey, who at first reviewed Wordsworth's poetry unkindly but later began to respect him as a writer; and Thomas De Quincey, who for twenty years after his *Confessions* lived on at Dove Cottage, wrapped up in his opium dreams. The remainder of the house is decorated with period furniture and a few portraits indirectly associated with the family.

(Wordsworth House is open Apr.–Oct., Mon., Tues., Wed., Fri., Sat. 10:30–12:30 and 2–5; Thurs. 10:30–12:30. Nominal charge.)

CONISBROUGH   (South Yorkshire): 5 mi. SW of Doncaster on A630

Conisbrough Castle, where Scott set some scenes of *Ivanhoe,* is noted for its magnificent twelfth-century keep with six buttresses and solid round towers, among the earliest of their type in England, all of which are intact and have required little restoration.

The environs of the castle bear little resemblance to scenes of the novel, however. Since Scott's time Conisbrough and its surrounding valley have become highly industrialized, and the castle is now set amid modern collieries and factories. Admirers of Scott should really visit Kenilworth (see entry), an ancient castle which crowns the top of lush green woods.

(Conisbrough Castle is open May–Sept., weekdays 9:30–7, Sun. 2–5:30; the rest of the year it closes an hour earlier. Nominal charge.)

CONISTON   (Cumbria): 8 mi. S of Ambleside on A593

By the time John Ruskin bought Brantwood for his summer home, he was already one of the leading literary figures of the Victorian age, having proven himself with the *The Seven Lamps of Architecture* and *The Stones of Venice.* Gradually he set up his priceless collection of books and manuscripts in the study and drawing rooms, and lined all the walls in the house with drawings of his own as well as by the Old Masters and Pre-Raphaelites. In his study and bedroom, for example, were a fine collection of Turner watercolors.

The curators of Brantwood have set up this house as a national memorial to Ruskin and a center for scholars of his work. Almost all of his drawings are on display either here or at the Bembridge School on the Isle of Wight; but here a special attempt has been made to reflect the development of his artistic genius, from the maps he began to sketch at an early age to his later architectural drawings and natural forms.

The pictures of Brantwood in the entrance hall are arranged to show the growth and development of the house. There are drawings of the original cottage, Ruskin's first drawing of the house in 1872, and studies by Joseph Severn and other artists. The drawing room has been hung with many pictures by Ruskin and a representative selection of his artist friends. Of special note in this room is his drawing of St. Mark's Square in Venice, and his copy of Botticelli's "Zipporah." The library houses some of the maps he made as a small boy and also some of his earlier architectural studies. On the shelves are first editions of the many prose works in which he dealt with the function of art in a social and economic context.

Ruskin's study has been decorated with objects relating directly to him. His self-portrait hangs over the fireplace, and there are several other pictures of him by friends around the room. A table where he worked during winters in London and the desk he used in the summer are here in addition to his favorite pieces of furniture. Among other items are his glass- and silverware, his inkwell and study candlesticks, and a large collection of books from his library.

Of special interest are the seven lancet windows of the dining room which Ruskin designed to represent the Seven Lamps of Architecture. Through them is a beautiful view of the Lake District. His own dining table and sideboard stand in the bay window. On the walls are portraits of Ruskin and his parents, and also one of his friend Thomas Carlyle.

In the coach house some interesting items reveal a bit of Ruskin's individual style. There is his boat, *The Jumping Jenny,* named after Nanty Ewart's brigin in Scott's *Redgauntlet,* and the double brougham coach which he had especially built to make the trip from London since he so detested the rail. But perhaps most amusing are his wicker bath chair and traveling bath, which he always had with him while away from home. On trips to the Continent the bath was always filled with books, and when riding by coach he attached it to the roof.

On the grounds are many paths Ruskin laid out, with vantage points for the best views. Considered the finest in the Lake

District, they have recently been redone to take visitors into the 250 acres of the estate which reach up to the top of the fells behind the house. In the woods are deer, red squirrel, and a wide variety of birds, plants, and unusual trees.

Back in the village of Coniston is a one-room **Ruskin Museum** with manuscripts, books, photographs, and personal relics which were once in Ruskin's home. A number of preliminary sketches for his major works, *Modern Painters* and *The Seven Lamps of Architecture,* are displayed here.

(Brantwood is open Mar.–Oct., Sun.–Fri. 10–5:30; rest of year by appointment only. Small entry fee. Ruskin Museum is open Apr.–Oct., daily 10–8. Nominal charge.)

COOLING   (Kent): N of Rochester on B2000, near Cliffe

If you're taken up by the desolateness of *Great Expectations* you ought to take a ride over the series of narrow, winding roads through the marshy farmlands of the Hoo Peninsula to Cooling. Dickens was said to have walked often the seven miles from Gad's Hill to Cooling, to gather material during the time he was writing the novel. The area is still bleak, and on a windy day rather spellbinding. **Cooling Churchyard** stands out starkly against the sparsely spread farms of the peninsula.

Just to the right of the entrance to the churchyard is a cluster of thirteen mounded stones, the graves of the eighteenth-century Comport children, who died within three years of each other. This scene probably gave Dickens the notion for the tombstones of Pip's dead brothers and sisters. Cooling residents also claim that he found the original of Joe Gargery's blacksmith shop at a farm that once existed here. (See Rochester entry.) They may have more support for their claim than the Dickensians of Rochester, since there was a small community here in Dickens' time and he was in the habit of taking scenes from the area.

A few miles down the road are the ruins of the ancient fortress **Cooling Castle,** said to be the home of Sir John Oldcastle, the original of Shakespeare's Falstaff. Though most of the outer wall is gone, the entrance and tower are still intact. On the site of the former keep is a modern house.

COVENTRY (West Midlands): 30 mi. SE of Birmingham

Nine hundred years ago Lady Godiva was said to have made her famous ride through the streets of Coventry. As a permanent reminder, a bronze equestrian statue of her stands on **Broadgate,** in the heart of the new Coventry which has been rebuilt since World War II.

According to legend, Lady Godiva was the beautiful and devout wife of Leofric, Lord of Coventry. When Leofric levied heavy taxes on Coventry, Godiva pleaded with him to relieve the townspeople of this extra burden. Leofric, so the tale goes, was unwilling to do so and therefore told his wife that he would relent on one condition, a condition he thought she would never fulfill—she ride naked on a horse from one end of the town to the other. Given her sense of duty to the poor, Godiva accepted the challenge and asked the townspeople to remain indoors, away from the windows. And so, with the streets deserted, Godiva rode upon her horse with her long hair covering her like a cloak. When she returned to her husband at the end of the ordeal, he made good his promise by abolishing the proposed tax.

Some versions of the tale say the ride took place when all the people of the town were assembled. Another possible explanation is that Leofric challenged her to ride stripped of her finery and jewels, as humbly as an ordinary citizen, and that the phrase "stripped of her finery" was reduced to plain "stripped" or "naked."

When Godiva died on September 10, 1067, according to historian William of Malmesbury, she was buried alongside her husband in a Saxon church on the site of the medieval diocese of Coventry.

COXWOLD   (North Yorkshire): 7 mi. SE of Thirsk

Shandy Hall's resident curator, a lifelong follower of Sterne, has collected a great number of objets d'art associated with the writer. Room after room is tastefully decorated with period furniture and works of art related to the novels. On the walls are prints of illustrations by Bumberry from *Tristram Shandy,* as well as the original Leslie oil of Uncle Toby and Widow Wadman. In beautiful eighteenth-century cases and shelves are the smaller incidentals.

With its massive stone chimney, winding corridors, and twenty rooms of odd shapes and sizes, it rivals *Tristram Shandy* in originality. Every attempt has been made to accentuate those features of the house which reflect Sterne's personality. Very recently the Lawrence Sterne Trust restored the house to its original state, even to removing oak paneling and drying it. In so doing they found such unique features as the massive kitchen fireplace with a room behind it, Adam fireplaces, and the parlor's elegant corner cupboard. Readers of the novel will appreciate attention to such details. The original structure, perhaps a much smaller dwelling, goes back much further than Sterne's time, however. During the restoration a medieval wall painting was found behind the parlor's oak paneling. It is thought that the house may have been a monk's dwelling, since there are ruins of an early monastery a few hundred yards away.

Sterne came to live here in 1760, when he became Coxwold's parson and needed a place to rent. It is not certain whether the house was named after his famous novel or whether it had previously been called Shandy (in Yorkshire dialect, "eccentric") because the house was a bit oddly constructed.

By the time Sterne came here the first part of *Tristram Shandy* had made him a literary success. The parsonage he took only as added financial security. Reportedly, he despised the church and found rural life distasteful, though he was a gifted preacher and his sermons were widely acclaimed in more metropolitan areas such as York. Though he spent quite a bit of time away from Coxwold, dealing with publishers in London and traveling on the Continent, he wrote the last seven volumes of *Tristram Shandy* and the whole of *Sentimental Journey* here. His study, restored as far as possible to its original state, has been turned into a library for Sterne scholars.

Sterne has allegedly returned to Coxwold's churchyard. Several years ago, when his London grave was doomed to be covered over by a new housing development, members of the Sterne Trust legally exhumed his body, verified its identity by comparing measurements of the skull to those of the Nollekens bust exhibited near the rear door, and brought his remains back to Coxwold for a proper funeral.

(Shandy Hall is open May–Sept., Wed. 2–6.)

DORCHESTER   (Dorset): 25 mi. W of Bournemouth

Dorchester, capital of Dorset, is the ideal center from which to explore the Wessex of Thomas Hardy's novels. It was his home, it was the scene of many episodes in his stories and novels, there is a fine Hardy collection in the museum, and the town sits in the heart of a countryside with Hardy associations. Dorchester can be reached by direct train from London, and is about forty miles southwest of Salisbury, which appears as Melchester in his novels.

Nineteenth-century Dorchester is vividly described as Casterbridge in the novel *The Mayor of Casterbridge,* and a number of places in that work can still be seen. In Hardy's time the **Town Hall** was the Corn Exchange, where the yearly hiring fair was held. Here roving farmhands gathered to offer their services to farmers. Each would wear the emblem of his trade— a carter, a whip in his hat; a thatcher, a plait of straw in his hat. On the opposite side of the street is the seventeenth-century **Antelope Hotel,** where Lucetta first met Henchard. On **Swan's Bridge,** right at the bottom of High Street, the habitués, which Hardy considered the lowest of characters, idled away their hours. **Grey's Bridge,** a quarter of a mile to the east, was a hangout for shabby genteel men. In *Far from the Madding Crowd* it was also the spot where Fanny Robin rested the stormy night she made her way to the Union Workhouse, now the **Damer's Road Hospital,** where she died in childbirth. The barracks, where her lover Troy and the other soldiers stayed, were at the top of the hill across from the modern town library. The county jail, which figures strongly in both novels, is the large brick complex located behind the Corn Exchange on **North Square.** Mill Street was Hardy's "Mix in Lane," where a number of shadier characters such as Japp, Fermitty Woman, and Mother Cuxsome lived. Hardy himself lived from 1885 until his death in 1928 at **Max Gate,** the house he designed himself, which is set in on the left on the road to Wareham, just beyond the Trumpet Major Inn.

The countryside surrounding Dorchester is so filled with Hardy sites that if you are familiar with his works you may want to get detailed driving tours from the Dorset County Library. One of the chief tourist attractions in the area has always been **Hardy's Cottage** at Higher Bockhampton, the house in which he was born. This is reached by driving east on A35 for about three miles, where there is a marker on the road for the lane reaching the cottage. (Just before the turnoff for the cottage is a sign for Stinsford Church, which has a memorial window to Hardy. His heart is buried in the churchyard here.) Once at the parking lot for the cottage, take the lane at the left for a twenty-minute walk through Thorncombe Wood. In the birthplace cottage (open by prior arrangement with the tenant) is the bedroom where Hardy wrote *Far from the Madding Crowd,* the ladder under which his grandfather Hardy hid smuggled brandy kegs, and the "squint window" where he watched for excisemen. Probably this secluded hamlet was the home of the Yeobrights, Fairways, and Cantles in *The Return of the Native,* since it is described in the novel as the western valley of Egdon by Thorncombe Wood, and in his own first edition of the novel Hardy penciled in the word "Thornicombe" on the sketch map he drew for it. Also a number of the places in the novel are consistent with the area's topography.

You can reach the western margin of "Egdon Heath" through a gate at the end of the lane by Hardy's Cottage; and the Rainbarrow—where all the characters met at one time or another—can be reached by walking through the valley and then south to a point where five paths meet over a prominent ridge until the ground abruptly dips ahead, giving a view of the wide valley of the Frome. At this point the tumulus named Rainbarrow is seen on the right, "even a little ditch remaining from which the earth was dug." In Napoleonic times a beacon was kept ready on the barrow to be lit as a signal in the event of invasion. In the novel there is a constant bonfire there.

Many scenes from *Far from the Madding Crowd* can be found in and around **Puddletown,** a bit farther east on A35. The road to Puddletown (Weatherbury in the novel) rises up Yellowham Hill (Yarbury in fiction). It was near the crest that Troy and Bathsheba met Fanny Robin as they returned from market. On the porch of Puddletown Church, Troy spent the night. Behind the ancient church Fanny Robin was buried, her grave "screened to a great extent from the view of passers from the road." Inside the church are many of the features Hardy mentioned—the gallery, the old pew boxes, and the alabaster effigies of the Martyrs.

In the novel, Bathsheba's farmhouse was on a hill to the west of the church; however, the house on which he based his architectural description is more than a mile away. This is **Waterston Manor,** which has been used in film versions of the novel. It can be reached by taking the A354 toward Blandford and then turning left onto B3142. Climb up the embankment just across from the entrance for a spectacular view of the manor and surrounding countryside. **Druce Farm,** thought to be the model for Farmer Boldwood's home, is about a mile away, back toward Puddletown at a point where the road divides three ways. Its stern bourgeois facade is an interesting contrast to Bathsheba's elegant manor.

At **Bere Regis** (Kingsbere), "a little one-eyed, blinking sort of place," is the church where Tess Durbeyfield and her family set up their four-poster bed, under the Turberville window in the south wall. Inside the church the tombs, "their brasses worn from the matrices," are still visible. Under a black flagstone bearing an inscription is the entrance to the Turberville vault. The family had come here with their wagonload of household goods after having been forced to sell their house in Marnhull. It must be remembered that Hardy was a trained architect and was often especially attracted to churches. Later in his life he restored one on the Cornwall coast.

Farther on in the town you can see the remnants of the **Woodbury Hill Fair,** which figured in many Hardy novels. This can be reached by turning right onto A31 at the town center, and then taking the small road that leads up Woodbury Hill. At the highest point in this road is a brick house. The gravel track on the left was the main thoroughfare of Woodbury Hill Fair. Part of the ramparts of an ancient earthwork can be seen immediately on the left. Formerly there were many permanent buildings as well as wooden standings and canvas tents on the open summit. Farther on past the old iron cattle grid the sheep fair was held.

Another village about ten miles north of Dorset figures largely in *Tess of the D'Urbervilles.* That is **Marnhull Marlott.** Some see the attractive Tess Cottage at Walton Elm, on the outskirts of Marnhull, as the original of the Durbeyfields' home. Others claim it is the present Blackmoor Vale Inn one mile northwest of the church. The "Pure Drop Inn" of the novel, now The Crown, stands near the main crossroads of the village opposite the church, and the field where the clubwalkers danced was, from Hardy's description, close by. It was on the road which leads past the Crown Inn to Shaftesbury (Shaston) that John Durbeyfield met Parson Tringham, the antiquary.

Jude the Obscure is largely set in **Shaftesbury,** even farther north. This hilltop town (Shaston in the book) was the home of Sue Bridehead after her marriage to Phillotson. When she rejoins Jude, the stonecutter, they travel far beyond the boundaries of Dorset and finally reach Oxford, "Christminster."

(Hardy's Cottage is open by appointment with the tenant for a small entry fee.)

DOVER   (Kent): at junction of A20, A2, and A258 on SE coast

Matthew Arnold's widely anthologized poem "Dover Beach" has imprinted a vision of pure white sands and high cliffs on the minds of many. Though railroad tracks run along the water and the port of Dover is within a mile, this area is still remarkably tranquil. On the empty fields above Shakespeare's Cliff at the eastern end of the beach, King Lear had his bout with madness and died trying to revive his hanged daughter, Cordelia.

DOWNE (Greater London): 7 mi. SE of Bromley, off A233

Perhaps the single most influential publication of the nineteenth century, *The Origin of Species,* came out of this peaceful seventeenth-century Kentish farmhouse, **Downe House,** now maintained by the Royal College of Surgeons as a memorial to Darwin. In Darwin's day, Downe was a remote village. Undoubtedly the seclusion he found here and the freedom from financial worries, ensured by a generous legacy from his father, enabled him to work out at leisure the theories that revolutionized thinking in the Victorian age.

The old study where he did most of his research and experimenting and wrote *The Origin of Species* has been reconstructed as nearly as possible to what it was during Darwin's lifetime. Near the window is the iron-frame armchair in which he often worked with board over his knee. Scattered over the large table and mantelpiece is the array of bottles and vials used for the constant experiments, and on the window shelf his microscope sits on the spot where he often used it. Many of the books filling the shelves and cupboards of this room are from Darwin's own collection, though the bulk of his library was donated to Cambridge University.

The drawing room, restored as closely as possible to its appearance when the family was in residence, contains furniture, pictures, and other objects in use during his lifetime. Here is the grand piano on which Mrs. Darwin played for her husband; also a number of family portraits and mementos. The Charles Darwin Room, also a drawing room at one time, contains a number of photographs, personal effects, and papers. There are notebooks he kept during his voyage into the Galápagos

Islands, whose unusual fauna provided much of the foundation for his views on evolution. Among the letters displayed are those written by Darwin to Karl Marx on the latter's work *Das Kapital*. One display case contains a number of his scientific instruments—a microscope, scales, a gyroscope—and also a large volume of notes on personal matters and various botanical experiments. On the center table is the announcement of the theory of evolution.

The room Darwin used as a study near the end of his life has been entirely redone to demonstrate, largely by means of mural paintings, the various stages in the process of evolution, and to note the scientists and philosophers whose discoveries led up to Charles Darwin's views on the subject in 1859.

Outside the house much of the garden remains as Darwin knew it. The Sandwalk encloses a little wood he planted with various trees and bordered on one side with holly. At the end there used to be a little summer house. This became the customary place for Darwin's daily exercise and was known as his "thinking path," for here he planned his work in his head as he walked.

(Downe House is open daily except Fri.; closed holidays. Small entry fee.)

DUMFRIES   (Dumfriesshire): 30 mi. NW of Carlisle

Burns House: Here Robert Burns came to spend the last three years of his life, after he had become established as a poet and exciseman and had more or less given up farming. During those last years at this house he wrote almost one hundred songs, among them "Auld Lang Syne" and "Ye Banks and Braes o' Bonnie Doon." Most of them were penned in his study, the small room off the bedroom. An autograph he scratched on the window with a diamond ring is still preserved there.

Burns's bedroom is furnished as it was when he died there, on the same day that his last son, Maxwell, was born. Beside his bed is a sketch of the room as it was then. Over the mantel is an etching of his inauguration into Canongate Kilwinning

Lodge in 1787, with pictures of his many acquaintances. The other upstairs room contains some of his personal books, among them Allan Ramsay's and Anna Seward's poems, which certainly had an influence on his own poetry. Among other items are the original manuscript of "Silver Tassie," his exercise book, and a number of mementos presented by various Burns societies around the world. At the top of the stairs is a life-size statue of Burns which was unveiled in Greyfriars Square in April, 1882.

The downstairs drawing room contains personal effects of his wife, Jean Amour, and such domestic items as the family toddy kettle and drinking glasses. On the walls of the kitchen and sitting room are many prints made from illustrations of his works.

At the **Burns Mausoleum** in St. Michael's Churchyard, a few blocks from Burns House, is the tomb of the poet, his wife, and their five sons. Fifteen years after Burns had been buried in an obscure grave behind St. Michael's Church, his Dumfries admirers built this elaborate tomb in the form of a Greek temple and moved him to it.

Also nearby is the **Globe Inn,** one of the poet's favorite drinking hangouts. The decor and clientele of this smoke-stained, oak-paneled tavern haven't changed much since his time. Visitors are still expected to sing and join in the merriment.

(Burns House is open Apr.–Sept., weekdays 10–1 and 2–7, Sun. 2–7; Oct.–Mar., weekdays only, 10–2, and 2–5. Nominal charge. Burns Mausoleum is open by arrangement with the curator.)

EASTWOOD (Nottinghamshire): 8 mi. NW of Nottingham

Eastwood, like Hardy's Dorset, is one of those areas which contains an author's entire frame of reference in a few square miles. Though the collieries have been modernized and there are more rows of red-brick miner's houses, the town's basic character has not been greatly altered since D. H. Lawrence described it. His haunts, especially those right within the town, can most efficiently be seen during a walk of an hour or so, and the best place to start is right in the middle of the business district, at the corner where the main road meets Victoria Street. Down the hill on the left stands **8a Victoria Street,** Lawrence's birthplace. This was a bustling commercial area in his day, and his mother supposedly used the bay window of the house for a small linen-and-baby-clothes business which she kept to supplement her husband's income from the mines. When he was two years old the family moved to 28 Garden Road, where he lived with his family until going away to school.

Farther on down the hill and across Scargill Street is an area of low brick houses which Lawrence called "the square" in *Sons and Lovers.* These and the similar rowhouses on Princes Street were built by the colliery company for its employees in the early 1840's and are very typical of the houses Lawrence described. Miners' children still romp in the narrow streets and soot-covered men in dark overalls plod home wearily after each shift is over.

To the right, at the end of Princes Street, a footpath leads across Wood Street and eventually down to **28 Garden Road,** his childhood home. The perception of Eastwood he had from that house and its immediate surroundings stayed with him for the rest of his life. This block of houses he immortalized in *Sons and Lovers* as "the Bottoms." Lawrence described the houses just as they are now, "very substantial and very decent," with little front gardens, little porches, and privet hedges. On the inside, the main room, the kitchen, was at the back of the house, overlooking the little back gardens, the ashpits, and the alley, "Where the children played and the women gossiped and the men smoked. . . ." You can easily picture Mrs. Morel carrying the ashes out, pumping water, and gossiping over the fence. The only modern additions are electrical wires and pipes for indoor plumbing which run up and down the sides of the houses. As of this writing the Young Writers Association is renovating the house as a memorial to Lawrence and will include a public museum.

Across from 12 Garden Street an asphalt footpath leads back up the hill to **Walker Street.** From the top of the hill you can scan the whole valley which Lawrence often referred to as "the country of my heart." He once told a friend that he knew this view better than any in the world and attested to the great impression it had on him. The setting of nearly all of his novels can be seen from this spot.

Just up to the right, about fifty feet to the left of the corner of Walker and Nottingham roads, stands the **Three Tuns Public House.** This was the Moon and Stars of *Sons and Lovers* where Walter Morel stayed and was seen " 'elping Anthony" during the wakes and fairs held in front of the inn. From here Nottingham Road goes to the right to reach the town center. This is a good point at which to circle back into town and pick up a car.

Farther on down Walker Street is **Lynncroft Street** on the right. The Lawrence family lived at No. 97 from 1902 to 1910. Then, about half a mile down on Walker, where Dovencote Road turns off to the left, stands the Beauvale Board School, which Lawrence attended before winning a scholarship to Nottingham High School. In *Phoenix I* he wrote about how he and his friends hated school "because they felt captives there . . . this was what they waited for: to go down to the pit, to escape, to be men." The school is a fancy Victorian building, with cupola and latticelike windows, a tall chimney. Just beyond the school is the modern Ram Inn. The original Ram Inn of *The White Peacock* is No. 46, the white house almost opposite.

There are also several places of interest on **Nottingham Road,** which swings around the town center from the Lawrence house back down the hill at 28 Garden Road. (Greenhills Road right beside the house becomes Mansfield Road and then Nottingham Road.) The large house on the left, at the junction of Greenhills and Mansfield roads, was formerly the colliery company office where Paul Morel collected his father's wages in *Sons and Lovers*. Also on the left is Miner's Welfare, formerly the Mechanic's Institute, whose lending library was often used by Lawrence and his friends. The market described in several of his stories was held at the Nottingham Road-Mansfield junction next to the Sun Inn. Opposite Mansfield Road at this junction in Church Street, and at its lower end, is the cemetery with the graves of the Lawrence family. (D. H. himself is not buried here. His ashes are in a tomb in Taos, New Mexico, where he lived in the early 1920's.) The inscription on his stone in the Lawrence family cemetery in Eastwood states simply, "Unconquered."

Greenhills Road leads down into Lower Beaudale and Engine Lane, and just over the railway level crossing is **Moorgreen Colliery**, the "Minton pit" of *Sons and Lovers*. The main road, B600, goes left and Moorgreen Reservoir is a short distance in on the right. In Lawrence's time there was a deep expanse of water here, and the drowning tragedy of *Women in Love* is based on an actual happening at this scene. He called it Willey Water in *Women in Love* and Nethermere in *The White Peacock* and *Sons and Lovers*: ". . . gray and visionary, stretching into the moist, translucent vista of trees and meadow," the lake was said to have been loud with birds piping one against the other and the mysterious splashing of water.

Perhaps the most sensuous of Lawrence country can be seen by taking a public footpath which starts from the lodge and leads to **Felley Mill**. (This is a delightful walk but in wet weather extremely muddy.) Near the lodge at the first bend in the road on the left is Lamb-Close House, featured in a number of Lawrence's stories as the house of local gentry. The long, low old house is Shortlands, home of the Criches, where the wedding party gathered in *Women in Love*, and High Close in *The White Peacock*. Lawrence described it as "spread along the top of a slope just beyond the narrow little lake of Willey Water"; it "looked across a sloping meadow."

A few yards beyond the junction of B600 and A608 is Felley Mill Lane (South). The gated road to Haggs Farm is blocked off by a private property sign, but you can get a glimpse of the farm where Lawrence claimed to have gotten his first incentive to write. Haggs Farm was the home of the Chambers family, whose daughter Jessie was engaged to Lawrence and who had a strong influence on his life and writing. She was immortalized as Miriam Leivers in *Sons and Lovers* and Haggs Farm in that novel was called Willey Farm. He described the cluster of low red farm buildings where Mrs. Morel and Paul hastened about, the apple orchard, the pond, and the cows who sought shade under the trees.

Down Felley Mill Lane is a road to the right which leads to

the derelict Felley Mill Farm, the Strelley Mill area of *The White Peacock*. It was suffering from old age even in Lawrence's time, the dark trees and weeds crowding out growth, keeping wind from flickering through.

From here you can return to Eastwood by taking the main road back to Underwood and then the A608 road to Eastwood via Brinsley. At that point there is a bus back to Eastwood from Underwood (the B3 or B6 via Brinsley).

The picturesque village of **Cossall,** four miles southeast of Eastwood, is the Cossethay of *The Rainbow* and can be reached by taking the 610 toward Nottingham and turning right on the A6096 road, through Awsworth to Cossall Marsh, which leads to the village. Marsh Farm no longer exists, but you can see the canal, the church, and the cottage—the honeymoon cottage of the Brangwens. The red, squarish cottage with its low slate roof and low windows stands next to the church under the old, dark yew trees. From there Will Brangwen peeped out of the white clockface on the tower to announce that there'd be no need for a clock.

The cottage, in actual life Church Cottage, was the early home of Louie Burrows, to whom Lawrence was engaged for a time. Her father, Alfred Burrows, was the model for Will Brangwen in *The Rainbow*. The church had wood carvings by Alfred Burrows and windows dedicated to the Burrows family.

The new **Nottingham County Branch Library** at Eastwood has a special room for its collection of books by and about Lawrence. But Lawrence scholars should go to the **Nottingham City Library,** Sherwood Street in Nottingham, which has the largest collection of printed and illustrated materials on Lawrence to be found anywhere. The library has been working on this and on a Byron collection for about twenty years. Among the materials available for qualified scholars is a series of forty tape recordings of persons who knew Lawrence, including Rebecca West, Aldous Huxley, and Bertrand Russell. The library also has a copy of the first Lawrence story ever to appear in print, "A Prelude," published in the Nottinghamshire *Guardian* under Jessie Chambers' name.

(D. H. Lawrence House is open by appointment.)

ECCLEFECHAN (Dumfriesshire): 5 mi. SE of Lockerbie, on A74

Carlyle's Birthplace: This arched eighteenth-century house, where Carlyle was born in 1795 and lived for the first four years of his life, is on the left side of the canal in the small village of Ecclefechan. Most of the furniture in the house was owned by the Carlyle family. In the kitchen-sitting room is his father's clock, still in working order. On the back wall is a sketch of the author's funeral procession in Ecclefechan. Carlyle came back as one of the most prominent men of his century.

The upstairs rooms contain a few personal effects—his cradle, traveling desk, and writing materials—but there are no manuscripts or important papers here. This house concentrates on his early family associations rather than his writing achievements.

(Carlyle's Birthplace is open Mar.–Oct., Mon.–Sat. 10–6.)

EDINBURGH (Midlothian)

Lady Stair's House has a comprehensive display of manuscripts, holograph letters, personal possessions, portraits, and other exhibits of three noted Scottish writers—Robert Burns, Robert L. Stevenson, and Sir Walter Scott. The house, built in 1622, is interesting architecturally because of its turnpike stairway and old dining hall. The Burns and Scott collections here are only of general interest, however, since the most important relics are housed at those writers' respective homes.

In the main hall the focal point is Scott's tall writing desk, a monument to his application and industry, at which he stood for many hours at a time correcting proofs. Here also are some amusing relics, among them a razor which belonged to Scott's great-grandfather, Beardie C. Scott. This old gentleman was such a fervid Jacobite that when King James VII of Scotland, actually James II of England, was deposed in 1688, he vowed never to shave again until the Stuarts were restored to the throne. More appealing is the battered old rocking horse that belonged to Scott as a child. It had footrests on different levels on account of Walter's lameness.

In the Burns collection on the second floor are many prints made from illustrations of "Tam O'Shanter" and "The Cotter's Saturday Night." There are also oil paintings of scenes from "The Jolly Beggars," that bacchanalian piece of poetic imagery. In the collection is Burns's letter to "Clarinda" (Mrs. Maclehose), who inspired the immortal song, and alongside it a lock of Clarinda's hair, as well as similar locks of "Chloris," "Highland Mary," and his wife, Jean Amour. Here also are a number of odd personal relics—a cordial glass with twisted stem, snuffboxes, the sword stick Burns carried as an excise officer. This personality is quite different from Scott's with his chessmen, pens, meerschaum pipe, or arty Quartier Latin bonnet.

The Robert Louis Stevenson collection is the most original. All the material relating to this author was recently brought here from his birthplace at **8 Howard Place,** which until recently was open to the public. It centers largely on Stevenson's relationship with his family, and especially his nurse, Cummy. The lifelong correspondence between these two is on display. The exhibit is divided into four parts: personal relics, relics of family and friends, letters and portraits, and many photographs from his years of travel.

Stevenson wrote *A Child's Garden of Verses* as a sickly child when he lived with his parents at **17 Heriot Row** here in Edinburgh. With its own private gardens, Heriot Row is still one of the most pleasant streets in the city. Here is the background of Stevenson's childhood, many aspects of which were incorporated into his book of poems. No. 17 faces south, and across the road are the gardens Stevenson used to play in. They must have seemed immense to a small child. From the street corner you can see the impressive outline of the castle. On a winter's evening in his day, old Leerie would come round to light the gas lamps as the gray dusk fell on the city. Many of his poems were also inspired at **Colinton,** three or four miles from the center of Edinburgh. Here, at the Manse, lived Stevenson's maternal grandfather. Colinton has changed a bit, but the Manse still stands on the "sleeping lawn" and the Water of Leith still dances on its way through the thickly wooded glen.

At **39 Castle Street** Sir Walter Scott worked when he was in Edinburgh. His biographer claims that he wrote the last two of the Waverley novels here. His boyhood house was **25 George Street,** at the top of Guthrie Street, off Chambers Street. A stone scroll marks the side of the house on College Wynd where he was born in 1771.

In **Braid Place,** a drab little street off the thoroughfare known as Causewayside, is a working-class tenement that was once Sciennes House, notable as the scene of the only meeting between Robert Burns and Walter Scott. That meeting, in 1787, has been recorded on a famous oil painting which hangs at Scott's home in Abbotsford. Through the passage at 7 Braid Place is the "back-green" where the plaque commemorating this meeting is now placed.

(Lady Stair's House is open June–Sept., Mon.–Sat. 10–6; Oct.– May, 10–5. Free.)

ELLISLAND FARM   (Dumfriesshire): 6 mi. NW of Dumfries, between A76 and River Nith

Robert Burns leased **Ellisland Farm,** a hundred acres on the west bank of the River Nith in 1788, having been totally captivated by the scenery. At that point Ellisland was an exhausted, runrig open pasture, and all his attempts to improve it by new agricultural methods failed. After a year here he was forced to take on an extra job as an exciseman, which involved his traveling on horseback up to two hundred miles a week in all weather. At the same time he tried to run the farm, gradually switching from livestock to dairying, and also continued to write. Finally, in 1791, he gave up farming as an "altogether ruinous business" and left for Dumfries to take up another post as exciseman.

A number of relics assumed to have belonged to Burns are displayed in the farmhouse, and the scenes of many of his poems are pointed out on signposts. "Tam O'Shanter" was written while he was pacing up and down what is now Shanter Walk, and visitors are able to see the field in which Burns saw the wounded hare which inspired the poem of that name.

(Ellisland Farm is open free all year.)

ELSTOW (Bedfordshire): 5 mi. S of Bedford

Elstow, where John Bunyan conceived *Pilgrim's Progress,* his allegorical account of the development of a Christian soul, remains much as it was in his day. In the fine old church is his baptismal font and the pulpit from which he preached the sermon on Sabbath breaking which so haunted his mind.

The church overlooks the **village green,** where Bunyan was playing tipcat when he suddenly beheld a vision which put him "into an exceeding maze," while a voice from heaven threatened him with hellfire if he did not mend his ways. This vision altered the course of his life. The immediate result was a long period of struggle to renounce the pleasures he enjoyed, among them bell ringing and dancing on the village green.

The village green and the half-timbered Moot Hall were the center of the yearly Elstow Fair, on which Bunyan based his colorful description of "Vanity Fair." The wicket gate through which Christian passed as he set forth on his pilgrimage was suggested by the gate leading to the church, and from across the wide field beyond came Evangelist to direct him on his way.

As a traveling tinker, Bunyan knew every nook and cranny of the district, and the characters in his book were based upon the people he used to meet on his journeys through the Bedfordshire lanes. In his day the roads were so bad that often he found himself plodding through thick mire, as he depicted it a "Slough of Despond on a gloomy day." Not far from Elstow lies **Stevington,** where water emerges from the Holy Well. Here, in his mind's eye, Bunyan saw Christian's burden fall from his shoulders and roll down the slope into the well.

It was when Bunyan was called to mend pots and pans at the Earl of Ailesbury's mansion on **Ampthill Heights** that he first glimpsed beautiful rooms, fine furniture, and rich carpets. Probably the view from the window, over the fields to the distant hills, was the inspiration for his Delectable Mountains. (Lidlington Hill, near Ampthill, is reputed to be Hill Difficulty.)

The actual House Beautiful of *Pilgrim's Progress* was nearby **Houghton House,** the Countess of Pembroke's home, built by Inigo Jones. It is now in ruins, but its staircase has been incorporated into the Swan Hotel in Bedford. (See also Bedford entry.)

EXMOOR   (Devon): the area N of Exeter

Readers of Richard Blackmore's *Lorna Doone* have long flocked to the wild and beautiful scenery of Exmoor, where that vivid romance is set. These North Devon and Somerset moors, with their deep-wooded combes and rugged, heathery uplands, have hardly changed since Blackmore wrote about them a hundred years ago. His story centers around the valley of the **Badgworthy Water, Hoccombe Combe,** and the villages of **Oare** and **Brendon,** all of which lie inland beyond a fringe of farms on the rugged coast of the Bristol Channel. Blakemore based the novel on a collection of Doone legends concerning a band of outlaws who descended on Exmoor about 1620, taking possession of several derelict dwellings. They terrorized the neighborhood, raiding, robbing, abducting women, and murdering—until, after a particularly vile murder, probably at Exford, they were driven from their lair around 1690.

The valley named Hoccombe on the map, at the western end of Badgworthy, is probably where the Doones lived. Blackmore made Oare Church the scene of John Ridd and Lorna Doone's wedding, and it was from the north window that Carver Doone shot Lorna. Nearby is Oare Manor, a gabled house, for many years the home of the Snowe family, who figure so prominently in the tale. Lorna Doone Farm, at Malmstead, stands beside Badgworthy Water with a packhorse bridge and ford.

From Oare a steep hill climbs up to the coast road running hundreds of feet above the sea along the fringe of Exmoor. To the south great stretches of open moorland dip and rise to the far horizon, dominated by Dunkery Beacon, the highest point of Exmoor. In the second chapter of the book, John Ridd describes the beacon light on Dunkery flaming at dead of night at the time of the first encounter with the villainous Doones.

Blackmore grew up in Exmoor. His grandfather was parson at Oare and he went to school at Blundell's in Tiverton, where the opening scene of the novel takes place with Jan Ridd's fight. The famous grammar school is a National Trust property, but unfortunately is not open to the public. Tom Faggus, the highwayman in the novel, was a real person and Blackmore heard many tales about him locally. He was a prosperous blacksmith in North Molton and had a marvelous strawberry-roan mare called Winnie. Lorna Doone, captive of a tribe of outlaws, and John Ridd, who attempted to rescue and marry her, are also thought to be real characters.

FELPHAM   (Sussex): just outside Bognor Regis

Blake's Cottage in this small coastal village is marked with a plaque. Here Blake often had mystical visions and wrote one of his greatest symbolic books, *Jerusalem*, which he illustrated with some of his finest engravings. Often when he had celestial visitants in the form of Joseph, the Virgin Mary, and others his wife would have to get up at night to sit quietly and calm him from his fierce inspirations.

GAD'S HILL PLACE   (Kent): just outside Rochester

Gad's Hill Place: Dickens spent the last fifteen years of his life at this large red-brick mansion several miles outside the city of Rochester. From his earliest childhood Dickens had admired the property, and when he was finally able to afford it in

1859, he had it furnished according to his tastes. In Dickens'
study, which is open during school vacations, is the series of
counterfeit book backs he designed to cover and conceal his
door. At the back is his touching memorial to "Dick, the best
of birds." The house is now a girls' school.

GLASTONBURY   (Somerset): 20 mi. S of Bristol on A39

The ruins of **Glastonbury Abbey,** serenely set among noble
trees and well-kept lawns, are all that remain of one of the
greatest monasteries in medieval England. After the abbey was
destroyed in 1539, during Henry VIII's dissolution of the
monasteries, the buildings were stripped and many of the stones
used to build the present town of Glastonbury. With a tourist's
map in hand you can readily reconstruct a vision of the abbey
five hundred years ago.

The rich legends saturating Glastonbury and its surrounding
meadows go back much further than medieval times. Glastonbury has long been identified as the ancient isle of Avalon,
burial place of King Arthur. In many works the folk hero
Arthur, generally accepted as the archetypal British general
who defended the lower part of the country from raiders, dwells
in the Celtic paradise of Avalon. Though William of Malmesbury's account of Glastonbury does not mention Arthur, a
number of old Welsh annals record his victories and place
his death in the year 516. His seat, Camelot, is thought to have
been the historic hill fort at nearby South Cadbury.

Arthur supposedly won a stunning victory at Badon Hill that
halted invading barbarians and permitted a rebirth of Celtic
arts to replace fading Roman influences. The village of **Badbury
Rings** in Dorset is traditionally thought to be the site of the
battle of Badon. Arthur may have been able to protect and ex-
tend the area under his control by using Roman cavalry tactics
against the Angles and Saxons, who fought better on foot.
Celtic youths, who traditionally sought out popular kings to
serve, would have flocked to Arthur's dragon banner, and he
could well have surrounded himself with a select company of

mounted companions, whose deeds would be sung by bards and minstrels. The king is said to have been mortally wounded on a battlefield called Camlann in a civil war against a kinsman named Mordred. He was then borne to Avalon and secretly buried.

In the twelfth century, when Geoffrey of Monmouth's book on the kings of Britain made interest in Arthur widespread, monks discovered a tomb said to have been that of Arthur and his queen, Guinevere, between two pyramids in Glastonbury's cemetery. Old church records say that in Arthur's grave a lead plate in the form of a cross was found with the inscription "Here lies interred in the Isle of Avalon the renowned King Arthur." The bones of the king were described as of great size, with the skull showing a wound. The matching casket contained, besides female bones, a scrap of yellow hair.

The two were soon after entombed in a shrine beneath the altar of the great church in the presence of Edward II. The base of that tomb was discovered in 1934, and their grave has since been indicated by markers.

Medieval literature is, of course, also rich with another legend, that of Joseph of Arimathea, who was said to have brought Christianity to England. There is a tradition that in A.D. 60 Joseph came from the south of France with his twelve companions to teach the Christian faith, and brought with him the chalice of the Last Supper or, in some versions of the story, phials holding the blood of Christ.

Chalice Well, or "the blood spring," is the chalybeate well said to have sprung from the spot where the sacred cup was buried. The waters became well-known as a spa during the early part of the nineteenth century and, along with a crypt in St. Mary's Chapel of the abbey, became a place of pilgrimage where miracles purportedly occurred. In the fourteenth century came the legend of the Glastonbury thorn, which supposedly blossomed miraculously at Christmas. Later it was said that the first tree grew out of Joseph's sword. That holly bush, the **Holy Thorn**, is located on the abbey grounds, next to St. Patrick's Chapel.

A climb to the top of **Glastonbury's Tor**, a 520-foot conical hill which forms a landmark for miles around, gives you a unique perspective on ancient Glastonbury and its legends. The tower of the Church of St. Michael, thought to have been built in the fifth century, is all that remains there, though the foundations of the church have been laid bare and its outline is easily visible. Several ancient carvings remain on the tower. One is a woman milking a cow, another the devil weighing the world against a human soul, and a third a pelican plucking his own breast.

The view from the top of the Tor is a complete panorama of the valley, from the Wiltshire Hills to the east and to Wells in the north. During Arthur's time this territory was much more swampy. The lake dwellers lived in huts which they built directly on the peat bogs. As their floors became damp, they built new peat layers on top. Many of the old huts found by archaeologists had as many as ten layers of flooring. Allowing for the magic of the Celtic imagination, you can easily imagine a barge gliding over one of the swamp's inlets, bringing King Arthur to Glastonbury for burial, or perhaps even an arm rising up out of the water, brandishing Arthur's sword Excalibur, which would assure the lake dwellers protection against a foreign foe. Ironically, archaeologists have discovered that all of this area's lake dwellers were massacred in a single battle. **Glastonbury Tribunal,** the medieval house on the main street of town which was the abbot's court during the time the monastery was in full operation, houses relics from that early period.

(Glastonbury Abbey is open June–Aug. 9–7, Sept.–May 9:30–sunset, daily. Nominal charge.)

GRASMERE (Cumbria): 5 mi. NW of Windermere

Wordsworth spent eight of the happiest and most productive years of his life at **Dove Cottage** in this small Lake District village. While he worked the earth and wrote, his sister, Dorothy, tended to the cottage and garden. During his stay here he wrote much of his finest work—the whole of *The Prelude* and some fine short poems, notably "Michael," "The Leech-Gatherer," and the "Ode on Intimations of Immortality." In his words, the Dove Cottage years were full of "plain living and high thinking," and one seemed to enhance the other. The love that he felt for his cottage and garden and the surrounding mountains and countryside is expressed constantly in his poems and Dorothy's *Journals*.

After Wordsworth married Mary Hutchinson, Dorothy remained with them at the cottage, until the coming of their three children forced them all to move out of their small quarters into a large house. From here they all went to nearby Allenbank and then down the road to Rydal Mount (see entry), where they stayed for the rest of their lives. Most of the furniture at Dove Cottage did belong to the family at one time or another and was brought back from Allenbank and Rydal Mount or donated by relatives.

As in most cottages, the principal room for daily living was the kitchen parlor, and that room remains as Wordsworth described it, with dark wainscoting from floor to ceiling, and his "perfect and unpretending cottage window with the little diamond panes," which looked over the garden of flowers and fragrant shrubs in summer and fall. This was the room to which Wordsworth came to rest and think after doing his work in the garden.

From the top floor you can get both the cozy feel of the cottage and the overwhelming feeling of the countryside which encloses it, since the cottage is built on the side of a hill with the back higher than the front. Up in the main sitting room Wordsworth often entertained his friends, among them Sir Walter Scott, Robert Jones (his traveling companion in Europe), and most of all Coleridge. In their time the view extended straight over the meadow and across the lake.

From the landing between the first and second floor you can look down over the gardens which were so important to Wordsworth. Great care is taken to stock the garden with the wild flowers, ferns, and mosses that are described in Dorothy's *Journals*.

After the Wordsworths departed, Dove Cottage was taken over by another literary great, their young friend Thomas De Quincey, author of the famous *Confessions of an English Opium-Eater*. The Wordsworths were pleased to leave the cottage in his hands, and De Quincey felt grateful to be living there. In his own words, "It was on a November night, about ten o'clock, that I first found myself installed in a house of my own—this cottage, so memorable to myself from all which has since passed in connection with it." Here he became a slave to opium, and had some happy years with his wife, Peggy Simpson, of Nab Farm. That farm's cottage, which sits up on a hill on the road to Ambleside, is now a guest house called Nab Cottage (see below).

In his *Confessions* De Quincey gives an intimate view of his stay here at Dove Cottage: ". . . . candles at four o'clock, warm hearthrugs, tea, a fair teamaker, shutters closed, curtains flowing in ample draperies on the floor, whilst the wind and rain are raging audibly without. . . ."

Just opposite Dove Cottage is **Wordsworth Museum,** constructed from an old barn adjoining Sykeside, home of the Wordsworths' servant Molly Fisher. It was opened in 1935 by poet laureate John Masefield to display literary material and objects of interest from the surrounding area.

On the ground floor is a model of a typical Westmoreland farm kitchen, furnished approximately as it would have been in Wordsworth's day. Also on display are many items which have been used by craftsmen of the area. The upper level, devoted entirely to Wordsworth, houses early manuscripts of *The Prelude* and the "Ode on Intimations of Immortality," the first surviving copies of Coleridge's *Christabel* and *Dejection,* and Dorothy's *Journals,* in addition to a number of first editions.

(Dove Cottage and the Wordsworth Museum are open Mar.–Jan., 10–1 and 2–4:15; Apr.–Sept., 10–1 and 2–5:45. Nominal charge.)

Nab Cottage, now "Nab Cottage Guest House," on the shores of the Rydal Water, was the home of both Thomas De Quincey and Hartley Coleridge, the eldest son of Samuel Taylor Coleridge, and himself an accomplished poet. The very sensitive young poet never recovered from his expulsion from Oriel College, Oxford, on a charge of intemperance, and he suffered a lifetime of melancholia and self-reproach. He was a well-known personality in the area, and was constantly seen wandering aimlessly and lost in thought—a figure of tiny stature with prematurely whitened hair and a character of charm, gentleness, and almost childish simplicity. Hartley Coleridge lies buried beside Wordsworth in the graveyard at Grasmere.

GUILDFORD (Surrey): 30 mi. SW of London

Guildford Museum: Lewis Carroll, author of *Alice in Wonderland,* died at a house called The Chestnuts, close to the Castle Gateway in Guildford, in 1898 and is buried in Guildford Cemetery. However, he never actually lived in Guildford. During most of the year he was Charles Lutwidge Dodgson, don and mathematics lecturer at Christ Church, Oxford, where he had his own living quarters with a study and personal library. The lease for The Chestnuts was in his name since he had secured the home for his six unmarried sisters after the death of their father, the rector of the Croft in North Riding, had left him the family patriarch. The north-country Dodgsons seem to have moved here because Lewis Carroll's childhood friend, the Rev. G. R. Portal, was rector at the nearby village at Albury. Until his death Carroll constantly made the trip up and down from Oxford to Guildford, usually for a few days at a time and for several weeks during the Christmas holidays.

It is said that the house was always bustling with activity and that nieces and nephews always begged to visit their aunts and uncle, who were very fond of children and had cupboards full of toys and games. Lewis Carroll, especially, was clever at inventing games and puzzles. In the Guildford Museum exhibit are cutout paper dolls made by his sister for one of the village children and several treasures from the nursery of the older Dodgson generation at North Riding. One is a history jigsaw of William IV's time and a "Wheel of Life."

The museum has a general collection of Carroll memorabilia on display but most of the valuable records and relics are in a special section, the Guildford Monument Room, and may be seen only by prior appointment. The collection contains childhood treasures, correspondence, and many photographs and sketches of Lewis Carroll and his family. Especially interesting to Carroll fans is a complete series of letters from Lewis Carroll to Mary Manners, a writer of children's books, and her brother Charles, a manufacturer of tin boxes in Mansfield. In one letter Lewis Carroll explains how he has tried for thirty years to keep the personalities of Carroll and Dodgson separate. Here also is a Looking Glass biscuit box, made by Charles Manners and very popular in Carroll's time.

The Lewis Carroll Society, which has its headquarters in London, has stocked the museum with the complete series of its quarterly publication *Jabberwocky* and is making an effort to build a library of Carroll material.

(Guildford Museum is open Mon.–Sat. all year; closed Sun., holidays. Free.)

HAMPSTEAD (Greater London): on London Underground

Poet John Keats first came to Hampstead to visit Leigh Hunt, who lived in the vale of Heath. Hunt introduced him to Charles Dilke, a civil servant, and Charles Armitage Brown, a bachelor, who occupied the semidetached house now known as **Keats House.** Before long, Keats, with his brothers Tom and George, came to live in Well Walk. A year later, after George had emigrated to America and Tom had died of consumption, Brown persuaded John Keats to live with him.

Until Keats left for Rome in 1821, this house was his home. Here he wrote his most famous works and became a partner in one of the most tragic romances of literary history. Soon after Keats arrived, Dilke rented his house to Mrs. Brawne, a widow with three children. Her eldest daughter, Fanny, then eighteen, became acquainted with Keats since they lived in adjoining houses and shared the same garden. The two became engaged, but Keats's early death in Rome in 1821 prevented the marriage.

The exterior of the house remains much the same as it was during the poet's time, with the exception of the drawing room added to the east side when the two houses were converted into one. The mulberry tree on the front lawn probably dates from Stuart times, but the old plum tree, beneath which Keats wrote his famous "Ode to a Nightingale," has been replaced.

Though Keats memorabilia are spread throughout the house, the sitting room is where he most often read and wrote. It has the original windows with their folding shutters and the shelves on which Keats kept his books. During his last illness he used to lie here on his sofa bed to watch Fanny in the garden or the gypsies out on the heath. Many of his letters to Fanny were written in this room.

The Chester Room, built after Keats's death, is used to house the Keats relics. In addition to some personal items, there are many books from his library: Shakespeare's poetry, Chaucer, *Anatomy of Melancholy,* and Livy's *Roman History.* Many of the books have his own poems transcribed inside the front cover. Here also is the original manuscript of Thomas Hardy's "At a House in Hampstead." Hanging on the walls are Joseph Severn's original sketch of Keats on his deathbed and the series of Hogarth engravings which Brown spent the whole winter of Keats's illness trying to copy. In Keats's diary are his own blistering comments on the project.

Upstairs on the wall of Keats's bedroom is a charcoal enlargement of Joseph Severn's portrait, inscribed "28 Janr. 3 o'clock mng—Drawn to keep me awake—a deadly sweat was on him all this night." Severn worked on this drawing while he sat at Keats's sickbed in their lodgings at the foot of the Spanish Steps in Rome. In this room at Hampstead, Keats supposedly saw his "death warrant," the spot of blood on the pillow which made him decide to take the trip to Rome.

The **Keats Memorial Library,** in the adjacent Heath Branch Library, contains extensive material relating to Keats and his contemporaries. Included are microfilm copies of all the Keats manuscripts, Keats material at Harvard University, and the holdings at the Keats-Shelley Memorial House in Rome.

HAWORTH   (West Yorkshire): 4 mi. SW of Keighley

The approach to the dark hillside village of Haworth—next
to Stratford, England's most popular literary shrine—is much
the same as Mrs. Gaskell described it over a century ago in her
biography of Charlotte Brontë. Though brick duplexes have
replaced some of the old cottages, you still climb up past the
Keighley mills, the endless rows of workers' cottages, up still
farther into the fells, and then finally to Haworth's steep cob-
blestoned **Main Street.** At the parking lot the village center begins, preserved almost exactly as it was during the
Brontës' time. Beyond the shops and the village blacksmith is a
square with the Black Bull, where Branwell Brontë spent many
evenings drinking, the drugstore which sold his opium, and the
Haworth Parish Church, successor to the Rev. Patrick Brontë's
church. Just beyond the myriad of horizonal slabs which make
up the cemetery is the **Brontë Parsonage Museum.**

Readers of the Brontë novels will be struck by the bleak
reality against which the Brontë sisters spun those passionate
and sensitive stories which were so far ahead of their time. The
family came here in 1820, when Patrick Brontë took over as
parson of the village church. Soon after her last child was born,
Mrs. Brontë succumbed to the consumption which was to wipe
out the lives of all six Brontë children before they could reach
middle age. Life at the parsonage was austere and isolated. A
Cornish aunt, Miss Branwell, came to keep house and taught
the girls needlework during the long winter afternoons when
walks to their favorite haunts out on the moors were impossible.
During the evening their father often read them tales of his
youth in Ireland, where he grew up in a log cabin, one of ten
children of a poor peasant farmer. The girls began to fantasize
early about the savage moors, and their Celtic minds began to
conceive the many stories of imaginary kingdoms that they recorded in the tiny homemade books now on exhibit in the
museum.

Their first contact with others took place when they began
to attend the Cowan Bridge School, the "Lowood School" of

Charlotte's *Jane Eyre,* which stood beside the Keighley–Kendal turnpike at Kendal Bridge. An account of those unhappy experiences is recorded in the novel. Lessons were very demanding and there were strenuous weekly trips, no matter what the weather, through the rugged fields to Tunstall Church, several miles away. The youngest girls, Maria and Elizabeth, were at the school for less than a year when they came home to die of tuberculosis.

Charlotte attended the Roe Head School until she was sixteen and there met Ellen Nussey and Mary Taylor, who were to remain her friends for life. It is from their extensive correspondence that most of the information about the everyday life of the Brontës has come. Charlotte returned to the school for a short time as a teacher, and for several years the remaining sisters—Charlotte, Emily, and Anne—were in and out of Haworth, trying jobs as governesses and teachers in various schools and homes. In 1842, Charlotte and Emily went off to Brussels to become more proficient at languages, with the hope of forming their own school, a project which never came to fruition, perhaps because their talents really did not lie in teaching.

Branwell Brontë had been the pride of the family in his youth, and great effort was made to have him develop the artistic talent so evident in his paintings. By the time he was twenty he had lost interest in such pursuits, becoming more and more irresponsible, forever losing jobs because of his drinking. As his consumption progressed he also became addicted to laudanum, which he was taking to relieve the pain, and spent most evenings at the Black Bull, charming the patrons with his witty stories. During the last few years of his life, when he was haunted by drink, opium, debts, and delusion, the inn was where he felt most comfortable. Only one person associated with the parsonage was close to Branwell then; that was the church sexton John Brown, father of the family's faithful servant. Branwell died in 1848 at age thirty-one.

Meanwhile the three sisters spent much time pouring out sadness in their soon-to-be-successful writing. Their first published work was a slim volume published under the pen names Currer, Ellis, and Acton Bell. Later, with Emily's strangely moving *Wuthering Heights,* Charlotte's *The Professor,* and

Anne's *Agnes Grey*, they used the same pen initials. Charlotte's
Jane Eyre became a success partly because of the adverse criti-
cism it received. The book was considered unconventional; its
straightforward views on female oppression and superficial social convention were thought out of the realm of propriety.
When the truth about author and location became known,
Haworth was immediately famous.

Emily and Anne were literary successes for only a short time
before succumbing to consumption. Then for about ten years
Charlotte lived on at the parsonage with her father. During that
time she penned her novel *Shirley,* which is largely based on the
personality of Emily. Just a year before she died she married
her father's curate, the Rev. A. B. Nichols, who remained at
the parsonage until her father, Patrick Brontë, died a few years
later.

During the time the Brontë children were growing up there
was no barrier of fir trees between the parsonage and the cemetery. The front windows of the house looked down on the
ever-increasing headstones and graves. Both Mrs. Gaskell, who
wrote a classic biography of Charlotte, and Ellen Nussey, whose
correspondence with the family has been preserved, described
the exterior as cold and austere. There was a gaunt Georgian
house with little shrubbery or gardens. The north and west
wings of the parsonage were added in 1872 by the parson who
followed Patrick Brontë, but aside from that addition and the
row of fir trees which separate the house and cemetery, the
scene is relatively the same as it was during the Brontës' time.

The first room on the left in the parsonage was the family
dining room, where Emily died on the sofa in 1848. The
Brontë Society has decorated it as it looked during Charlotte's
last years, when the income from her works enabled her to
spend some money on the house. According to her friend Ellen
Nussey, the rug, curtains, and wallpaper were not typical of
the decor during most of the time that the sisters were alive.
Patrick Brontë had always forbidden curtains owing to his
fear of fire, and they could never afford more than tinted wallpaper. Across the hall is the parlor, actually Patrick Brontë's
study and the place where he took his meals. Children were
allowed only by invitation. Mr. Brontë still peers over the room

from his portrait over the fireplace, and his spectacles, pipe, and tobacco box are laid out suggestively on the table. On the walls are watercolors by the Brontë sisters.

At the far right of the hall is the kitchen, where the girls learned to cook and do needlepoint. Here Emily is said to have baked bread while propping up her German books on the table. To the left is the old peat store where the Brontë sisters kept their two tame geese, Adelaide and Victoria. This room was later converted into a study for Charlotte's husband, A. B. Nichols.

The upstairs rooms reveal more of the Brontë children's artistic and literary activities. Many of their juvenile manuscripts were written in the nursery, and on the plaster in this room are a number of small drawings done by the children during their quiet play there. In a display case are some of their toys and pencil drawings. Charlotte's room, now filled with clothing and family portraits, was the room in which she died, after being married for only nine months. In Branwell's room are some examples of his art work, including copies of "The Pillar Group," a portrait of his sisters, and the profile portrait of Emily, now hanging in the National Gallery.

The exhibition rooms are filled with personal relics, a large portion of them Charlotte's. Prominently displayed are such items as Charlotte's favorite pink nightgown, her gray-silk going-away dress, and the bonnet she may or may not have been wearing with it. Downstairs is the famous Bonnell manuscript collection. Here are some of the tiny hand-printed books in which the Brontë children recorded their tales, the correspondence Charlotte had with her friend Ellen Nussey and with her publishers, and a canceled page from her last novel, *Villette*. In the adjoining library are photostats of the manuscript collection and many books about the Brontës and the Haworth moors.

Though the church the Brontës knew was torn down and rebuilt by Patrick Brontë's successor, the present church is filled with Brontë associations. All the family's births and deaths are registered here, and at times the register is open to the entry recording the marriage of Charlotte and A. B. Nichols in 1854. There is also a communion table from the old Haworth

Church, a stained-glass window commemorating Charlotte, and a memorial tablet marking the Brontë vault. The composite view of the church, the cemetery with its many slabs of dark, moldy stone, and the austere parsonage beyond it remind you of the desolateness the Brontës must have felt here.

There are a number of walks you can take from the parsonage and across the moors into Brontë country. The most popular is the walk to the **Brontë Waterfalls** and Top Withins. You can walk the entire way, about seven miles round trip, or go most of the way by car. Take the West Lane out of the village and make a left turn at a sign marked "Brontë Falls." To the right is the Hill Top Café. After crossing an intersection with the reservoir road, continue down to Far Intake. From Far Intake, which is as far as cars can go, a rougher road descends down to Sladen Beck and the falls. On the way is the famous Brontë chair, a large stone which stands upright in the form of a seat. Though the waterfalls are very small, this was a favorite haunt of the Brontë children and appears particularly in the prose and verse of Emily.

From here the walk to **Top Withins,** the speculated site of Emily's *Wuthering Heights,* is not far. Just over the Brontë bridge is a footpath which runs up the hillside, to the left of the ruined Virginia Farm on the horizon. In dry weather you can just walk straight ahead about a quarter of a mile and see Top Withins up the road. Another route is around the back of the Virginia Farm and through the yard of the next ruined farm to the track for Top Withins, which is behind a wooden gate across the road. For years Brontë lovers have made the pilgrimage here. A plaque on the wall of the ruined farmhouse notes that it has long been thought the Earnshaw house in *Wuthering Heights,* but that "the buildings, even when complete, bore no resemblance to the house she described, but the situation may have been in her mind when she wrote of the moorland setting of the heights." You can imagine Isabella's suffering in the house, and the golden cornfields, hayfields, and garden which once surrounded it. Some argue for Ponden Hall as the more likely location, since its rooms were laid out very much as those of Top Withins.

You need not walk all the way to Top Withins to get a feel-

ing for the moors that the Brontës had. There are derelict
farmhouses scattered over the high, windswept heath, and many
of them are very similar to the house in the novel. The moors
will remain untouched as a reminder of the Brontë novels. The
soil is too poor to grow crops, too marshy to build on, and too
cold and rainy to attract tourists. The vision of *Wuthering
Heights* becomes clear as one gets into this landscape: there is
nothing cultivated, nothing human, and nothing to feed the
imagination but the wind and clouds.

Ponden Hall, also the Thrushcross Grange of *Wuthering
Heights,* can be reached by driving to Stanbury and taking the
road that veers off to the left just after the Silent Inn. The
house stands on the right, almost on the edge of the reservoir.
The Brontë sisters knew the house well and referred to the five
shy Heaton bachelors who lived there as "the five brethren."
Two of the brothers were trustees of Haworth Church.

Wycoller Hall, the Ferndean Manor of *Jane Eyre,* is a beautiful gray-stone ruin tucked away in the hamlet of Wycoller. The
hall has been uninhabited for over a hundred years, and at this
point the roof has fallen in and the walls have crumbled. In
this tiny hamlet you can really slip back into the novel. There
are seven different little bridges built over the wooded stream
on the way to the hall. It is said that once a year a horseman
comes galloping full speed up to the front door as the wind is
howling loudly, and after abruptly dismounting makes his way
up to one of the rooms of the house. Dreadful screams of a
woman are heard, and as he gallops away on his steed, they
turn into progressively low groans. Legend says that the master
of the house had murdered his wife there and the horseman is
merely his ghost coming back to pay his annual visit.

Another hall which contributed much to *Jane Eyre* is **Norton
Conyers,** near Ripon. Charlotte made a social visit to the house
when she was employed as a governess by friends of the owner.
Here, more than with most of the halls she "borrowed," Charlotte described the hall almost exactly as it is in reality. Thornfield Hall in the novel also had a church at its front gate, an
oak-paneled hall covered with ancestral portraits, the broad
oak staircase, and the madwoman's room on the top floor. Here
she found the ideal ancient hall to combine with the legend of
the decaying Wycoller Hall.

Another house not far from Haworth is **Oakwell Hall,** which stands in the little village of Birdstall. Once inside, you will find several clues which leave no doubt that this beautiful sixteenth-century house is the original of Fieldhead, the home of Shirley in Charlotte Brontë's novel by that name. Just as described in *Shirley* are the wide old fireplace, the gallery, the latticed window, even the stag heads. To the left of the fireplace there is a door which leads to the kitchen, where Shirley, having been bitten by a dog she believes is mad, cauterizes the wound with a red-hot iron. (This episode is said to have been based on a real-life incident at Haworth when her sister Emily did the same thing.)

Today Oakwell Hall is open to the public as a period house. In the great hall where the Fearnleys and the Batts used to entertain their friends, concerts and dramatic performances based on scenes from the Brontë sisters' novels are sometimes held.

Slightly more than a mile away is the **Red House** at Gomersal, which was reached in the Brontës' day by "quiet hidden lanes." Today the area is much more industrialized, but Red House itself remains as it must have appeared to Charlotte when she made it the Briarmains in *Shirley*. She appropriated for her story not only the house but also the entire family then living there, the Taylors, who in the book became Hiram and Jessy Yorke and their children. The stained-glass purple-and-amber windows from this house are now on display at Haworth. Mary Taylor, the daughter of the real-life family at Red House, was a close friend of Charlotte's.

(Brontë Parsonage Museum is open Jan.–Mar., 11–5; Apr.–Dec. 24, 11–6. Nominal charge.)

HUGHENDEN (Buckinghamshire): 2 mi. N of High Wycombe on A4128

Hughenden Manor: By the time statesman and novelist Benjamin Disraeli was twenty-two he had already published *Vivian Grey,* one of a number of his political novels which appeared at intervals for over half a century. Through these works he was able skillfully to convey his own vision of New Toryism to a wide range of readers. He is remembered as a statesman for the brilliance by which he reformulated the Tory tradition and showed that the principles of Bolingbroke could be adapted to the changed circumstances of the industrial age. The main characters of his three major novels, *Vivian Gray, Sybil,* and *Coningsby,* were also projections of Disraeli personally. In each a young man mapped out a way that he could eventually become a respectable landed gentleman, just as Disraeli was to do by negotiating for Hughenden.

Disraeli bought Hughenden in 1847, when, as a potential leader of the Conservatives in the House of Commons, he felt that it was time for him to become a landed proprietor. He went deeply into debt to purchase the estate. In fact, it was fifteen years before he was able to model the house and grounds according to his own tastes. Upon the renovation of Hughenden he had achieved his goal. He too was living in the style of a Harry Coningsby, and working to effect those political ideals he had formulated early in his life.

Ten years after their arrival, the Disraelis wholly remodeled the house according to the taste of the period. It had been a simple eighteenth-century building of stuccoed appearance. They added Gothic decoration in and out, and made extensive changes in the garden and grounds. Mrs. Disraeli laid out a German forest with circuitous paths and rustic seats, and an Italian garden along the stone terrace. In due course the little pond was broadened into a lake and inhabited by two swans, Hero and Leander.

Almost every autumn, when Parliament was in recess, Disraeli and his wife retreated to their new property. He loved the fall and spoke of the many shades of the leaves at Hughenden which "come down at the first whisper of the frost" and "then go out like lamps when the dawn breaks on a long festival." He also loved the spring here, but often found himself mewed up in London at that time, longing to get back to watch the first breath of spring with the sultry singing of many birds.

Disraeli came to this country house often until his death in 1881, and was visited informally here by Queen Victoria in 1877. She lunched with the Prime Minister in the Gothic dining room and afterward planted a tree on the south lawn. The visit is thought to emphasize her gratitude to him for achievements during his ministry.

Near the end of his life, after his wife had died and his tenure of office had ended, Disraeli often came to Hughenden alone to wander around the gardens and spend time in front of the fire in his library. Though he died in London, he gave instructions that his body be returned here. He is buried beside his wife in the simple graveyard on the side of Hughenden Church, which is on the left of the lane winding up to the house from the main road.

(Hughenden Manor is open Feb.–Oct., Mon., Wed., Thurs., Fri. 2–6, Sat. and Sun. 12:30–6. Small entry fee.)

ISLE OF WIGHT

The Isle of Wight, with its impressive cliff scenery, thickly wooded ravines winding down to the sea, and delightful thatched-roof villages, was a haunt of Queen Victoria and the poet Tennyson, among others. **Osborne House,** near Cowes, was the royal residence for the last half of the nineteenth century and Victoria died here in 1901. The royal apartments are preserved exactly as they were in her time. Tennyson lived at **Farringford House,** now a hotel, near the western tip of the island, and for him the most convenient crossing to the mainland was from Lymington to Yarmouth. Traveling this route on a winter's evening in 1889, he conceived one of his finest poems, "Crossing the Bar."

Tennyson frequently took walks around the area near his home and it is still possible to follow the same path that he used to take from Farringford Hotel, near Freshwater Bay. It is said that he often fled into the woods to escape the prying eyes of visitors who used to besiege the house, and on one occasion actually fled from a flock of sheep, having mistaken them for a flock of his admirers.

Probably the finest coastal viewpoint is **Tennyson Down,** not far from the hotel, with its view below to the Needles, the three detached masses of chalk, guarded by a lighthouse on the western extremity of the island.

At the **Bembridge School** are the Ruskin Galleries, containing a large number of Ruskin's letters, manuscripts, drawings, and books. The school was founded at the turn of the century by an educator and Ruskin enthusiast. Here and at Ruskin's summer home in the Lake District (see Coniston) almost all of his original papers and drawings are housed.

KENILWORTH   (Warwickshire): 5 mi. SW of Coventry

Queen Elizabeth conferred **Kenilworth Castle** on her favorite Robert Dudley, Earl of Leicester, and here were enacted the pageants and lavish festivities described so vividly by Sir Walter Scott in his novel *Kenilworth*. By the time Scott came to know the castle it was a magnificent red-stone fortress in ruins. Since then dangerous sections have been restored and the ground inside landscaped, but the setting remains the same —a classic ruin set in beautiful green forests. It takes little imagination to lapse back into the novel.

The castle remained a royal possession until the Civil War, when the Parliamentarians set about its destruction, fearing it might become a stronghold of Royalist resistance. They demolished the north wall of the massive keep and divided the property into two parts. Despite the destruction and decay, much remains of the buildings—the great keep, King John's encircling wall, John of Gaunt's banqueting hall, and the gatehouse, which is now a residence. At the bottom of the hill is Long Barn, built in the sixteenth century, and in front of it a chapel of John of Gaunt's time.

King's Arms Hotel in the town deserves a visit. Here in 1815 Sir Walter Scott wrote many pages of the novel which was to make the name Kenilworth familiar in households the world over. The bedroom he occupied still contains the original furniture, including the four-poster bed in which he slept.

(Kenilworth Castle is open May–Sept., Mon.–Sat. 9:30–7, Sun. 2–5:30; closes an hour earlier rest of year. Nominal charge.)

KESWICK   (Cumbria): 20 mi. NW of Windermere

The collections in the small **Fitz Park Museum** in the heart
of the Lake District consist primarily of literary manuscripts
and rock formations from the area, plus a few sentimental relics
such as a lock of the aging Wordsworth's soft white hair,
Southey's gloves and flute, and Ruskin's court dress. Although
most of the material is Robert Southey's, there are also some
manuscripts and letters of Hartley Coleridge, Wordsworth,
Walpole, and Ruskin. Especially interesting is a letter from
T. E. Lawrence to Hugh Walpole in which Lawrence describes
his *Seven Pillars of Wisdom* as "part ponderous, part hysterical,
too long and very amateurish." Most of the papers have been
photocopied so that they can be read easily by visitors.

The museum centers around the "Friends of Robert Southey"
display, which contains Wordsworth's poems "Triad" and
"Wishing Gate," Hartley Coleridge's "To William Wordsworth
on his 75th Birthday," Thomas De Quincey's diary, and personal items associated with those authors. Perhaps the most
popular piece here is Southey's "Story of the Three Bears,"
published in *The Doctor* in 1848.

Southey, who often expressed his affection for Keswick in
letters and poems, described the view from the low hill near
Greta Bridge as "perhaps the finest single spot in England."
Greta Hall, where Southey lived for forty years and often had
Coleridge as a long-term house guest, is now the **Keswick School.**
Southey is buried in the churchyard at **Crosthwaite Church.**
This gaunt rectangular house was a home of happiness, with
many joyous hours spent in gatherings of the poets; but in later
years there was also a note of pathos. Here Southey edited the
works of Cowper, whose mental afflictions he sadly remembered,
while at the same time his wife, who had also suffered a mental
collapse, was slowly passing away.

(Fitz Park Museum open Apr.–Oct., 10–12, 2–5; closes 2 hours
later in July–Aug. Nominal charge.)

KIRKSOWALD (Ayrshire): 4 mi. SW of Maybole, on A77

Souter Johnnie's Cottage: The Souter Johnnie of Burns's poems was in real life John Davidson, cobbler of Kirksowald and drinking companion of the poet. Burns came here often during the time he was in Kirksowald, supposedly studying agricultural methods at Hugh Rodgers School. He admitted making some progress at his studies, but "I made much greater progress in the knowledge of mankind." He was reputed to have spent half the time drinking and the other half studying local women. This fits in with his legendary image as a ribald drinker and lusty man about town.

This cozy cottage, furnished as it would have been two hundred years ago, is a much more authentic slice of Burns's world than the large, relatively bare birthplace cottage on the now-built-up Main Street of Alloway. Kirksowald is still a small country village amid rolling hills, with the local hotel, post office, and general store its main gathering places. During Burns's time it was a center for contraband trade, and he mixed freely with smugglers like Souter Johnnie.

One room of the cottage is reconstructed as the cobbler's shop which John Davidson would have kept. In this room, in front of the window facing the town's main road, he and Burns spent many hours drinking and telling tales. The chairs and drinking table here are thought to be original. In the bedroom is a built-in bed which conceals a tunnel for smuggling in contraband goods from the backyard to an open space under the floorboards of the cottage.

The back garden, which in the cobbler's time provided potatoes and other vegetables for the household, is now laid out in grass. At its center are four life-size figures, carved in stone, of Tam O'Shanter, Souter Johnnie, the innkeeper of the local hotel, and his wife, as Burns must have visualized them sitting around the inglenook of the inn. The facial expressions and details of the garments worn by the four are amazingly detailed. Johnnie is diverting the innkeeper with ribald stories while

Tam seduces the man's wife with his eyes. The statues were
done by a self-taught Ayrshire sculptor, James Thom. Just a
block from the cottage is the **Kirkton Hotel,** where Burns did a
lot of drinking with those friends.

It was in Kirksowald that Burns supposedly found the materials for his famous poem "Tam O'Shanter," modeled after
Douglas Graham, tenant of the farm of Shanter, whom he had
met through Souter Johnnie. Graham often came into Kirksowald to drink the evening away, while his wife sat at home im-
patiently in her rocking chair, as Burns wrote, "gathering her
brows like gathering storm, nursing her wrath to keep it warm."
Local legend tells us that the story came to him one night after
he had taken Graham's boat, the *Tam,* out sailing to the nearby
Ailsa Craig and was forced back by stormy weather. When he
sought refuge at the Shanter farmhouse, he found Graham's
wife "waxed exceeding wrathful about her husband's out booz-
ing at a fair." It was then in anger that she prophesied the super-
natural tale of Tam O'Shanter and his perilous ride from the
inn at Kirksowald to Alloway.

(Souter Johnnie's Cottage is open Apr.–Sept., weekdays 2:30–6.
Nominal charge.)

KNEBWORTH   (Hertfordshire): 20 mi. N of London

Knebworth House is the ancestral home of Sir Edward
Bulwer-Lytton, Victorian novelist and close friend of Charles
Dickens. His most famous novels, *The Last Days of Pompeii*
and *Last of the Barons,* were written right in the library of
Knebworth House and were part of the seventy volumes of
novels, plays, poetry, and essays which made him one of the
great Victorian men of letters. There are associations with
Charles Dickens here too, and it was in the Banqueting Hall,
one of the surviving parts of the Tudor mansion which dates
back to 1492, that the two writers staged their highly successful
amateur theatricals.

An early picture of the house shows that it was a gracious
quadrangular brick building until 1811, when the mother of

the novelist began to renovate the house in the spirit of the Romantic Revival. During the first half of the nineteenth century three sides of the quadrangle were demolished, the yellow brick was covered with cement to look like stone, and the house was given a new and fanciful appearance with towers, battlements, copper domes, heraldic devices, and a profusion of gargoyles. As a result this old Tudor mansion has a split personality. As soon as you pass through the entrance doorway the character of the Gothicized exterior dissolves and the peaceful spirit of a centuries-old home takes its place.

Evidence throughout the house indicates that the lives of the Lyttons were devoted to literature, public life, and public service. Sir Edward Bulwer-Lytton, in addition to his prolific literary life, was a member of Parliament and a colonial secretary. His son, Robert, was a distinguished diplomat and the first Viceroy of India, and also a writer and poet who concealed his identity behind the name Owen Meredith. His own son, in turn, became a novelist.

The tour of the house begins at the splendid Banqueting Hall, with its early sixteenth-century ceiling, its minstrels' gallery and screen dating from about a century later, and all of its associations with Lytton-Dickens theatricals. You can easily imagine family and friends gathered here for drama productions and for the Christmas celebration, attended by everyone on the estate, with carol singers, logs blazing in the great open fireplace, and an enormous Christmas tree reaching almost to the ceiling.

Aside from the Banqueting Hall, the Library is perhaps the most impressive room at Knebworth. This is where Sir Edward wrote his books, and the blotter which he used to blot his last page is there on his desk, along with first editions of his works and several of his own manuscripts and those of his son and grandson. The portrait by E. M. Ward over the mantelpiece shows him as an old man, smoking one of the long pipes which were part of his image. Also on view are letters from Charles Dickens and programs of the "Knebworth Private Theatricals." In the cast list of Ben Jonson's *Every Man in His Humour,* the role of Captain Bobadil is played by Charles Dickens.

On the walls of the main staircase are a number of family portraits by Neville Lytton, together with his unusual portrait of George Bernard Shaw wearing the robes of a pope! The State Drawing Room remains almost exactly as decorated by Sir Edward. One wall is dominated by a large oil painting by Daniel Maclise, illustrating a scene in *Last of the Barons* and commissioned by John Forster, friend and biographer of Charles Dickens and also a friend of the Lytton family. It depicts Edward IV visiting Caxton's printing press and symbolizes a transition from the days of feudalism and chivalry to the new age of trade. The special point of interest in the picture is the armored figure of Earl Rivers, which is, in fact, a portrait of Sir Edward himself. Before the Victorian renovation of the house, this room was known as the Presence Chamber and was originally hung with tapestries. Queen Elizabeth I was received here when she visited Knebworth in 1588.

(Knebworth House is open Easter–Sept., Tues.–Sun. 2–5; park is open 11–6. Small entry fee to one or both.)

KNOLE (Kent): S of London on A224 to Sevenoaks; then follow signs

Knole is one of England's largest mansions. Built in 1456 by Archbishop Thomas Bourchier, the gaunt gray structure crowns the rounded hill, or knoll, from which it takes its name, near the ancient town of Sevenoaks in Kent. The three-acre house has a number of elaborate staterooms built for the kings and clergy who came here for several centuries. Henry VIII is especially remembered for the priceless tapestries and art galleries he brought. Legend has it that its seven courtyards correspond to the days of the week, its fifty-two staircases to the weeks of the year, and its 365 rooms to the days of the year.

Virginia Woolf became so enraptured with Knole on her visits here that she used it as the basis for her fantasy *Orlando,* in which she called it "a town rather than a house." Orlando sees Knole through the eyes of a painter. At one point he gazes through the labyrinth of passages and sees the many poets of Knole at work. At another time he looks at the house from one of his favorite vantage points and remembers the many generations of lords and servants whose love and toil have given it life and form. The original manuscript of *Orlando* is now on display in the Great Hall. Virginia Woolf gave it to her close friend Victoria Sackville-West in 1928 and it was later bequeathed to Knole.

Dryden, Pope, and Wycherley also made visits to Knole some three hundred years earlier to visit their friend Charles Sackville, the sixth Earl of Dorset, courtier of the Restoration, lover of Nell Gwyn, and a poet in his own right. He is said to have been a typical figure of the court of Charles II—witty, munificent, and rakish. Dryden dedicated his "Essay on Satire" to him, and also his "Essay on Dramatic Poesy," in which Lord Dorset figures under the name of Eugenius.

It is easy to imagine the gatherings this coterie must have had in the Great Hall, a fifteenth-century room with oak paneling, plasterwork ceilings, and a great number of carvings and heraldic emblems. Up above an elaborate oak screen is the Musician's Gallery, bordered by wooden lattices. This was where the private orchestra performed for the family and their guests, who sat at a long table on the raised platform at one end of the room. Down the main body of the hall sat the household at different tables arranged according to their occupations. There was the kitchen table, the clerks' table, the nursery table, the parlor table, the laundrymaids' table, and the long table, which is still here.

(Knole is open Apr.–Oct., 10–12 and 2–5, Nov.–Mar., 10–12 and 2–3:30, on Wed.–Sat. plus bank holidays. Closed Dec.–Feb. Admission charged.)

KNUTSFORD (Cheshire): on A50, 15 mi. S of Manchester

Knutsford is Elizabeth Gaskell's Cranford. Her memories of the small market town where she lived with a maternal aunt until her early adulthood provided the raw material for that endearing record of English provincial life in the 1830's and 1840's. *Cranford* is a gentle evocation of the gossip and the card parties, the small snobberies, and the good-heartedness of mid-nineteenth-century English provincial life. It is possible for readers of the novel to find many buildings that are familiar, some of them little changed since they helped form the background for Miss Mattie, Miss Pole, Mrs. Fitz-Adam, Captain Brown, and the other characters of the novel.

Still standing amid the old black-and-white timbered cottages of **King Street** is the Royal George Inn with its Assembly Rooms, where the conjurer Signor Brunoni mystified the Cranford ladies with his tricks (but not Miss Pole, who claimed to have the "receipts" for most of them). Not very far away, at No. 81, a chemist's shop occupies the former premises of the Cranford branch of the bank that failed, leaving Miss Mattie almost penniless. A note issued by the bank can be seen in the Public Library at the foot of Adams Hill. The library also contains a fine collection of the first editions of Mrs. Gaskell's works and some of her possessions.

The titles of her books, which include the famous biography of her friend Charlotte Brontë, are carved in stone on a wall of the Gaskell Memorial Tower in King Street, which also displays her portrait bust by D'Orsi.

Two roads in the town, **Gaskell Avenue** and **Cranford Avenue,** are named in her honor. No. 17 Gaskell Avenue was the home of Mrs. Lumb, the aunt with whom she spent most of her girlhood, and is thought to be the original of Mrs. Fitz-Adam's house in *Cranford,* that large rambling edifice which "had been usually considered to confer a patent of gentility upon its tenant, because, once upon a time, seventy or eighty years before, the spinster daughter of an earl had resided in it."

Marked with a commemorative plaque, No. 17 is a friendly-looking brick mansion overlooking the thirty acres of Knutsford Heath, where every spring the town's May Queen is crowned with great pomp and pageantry. Before the crowning there is a procession in which liveried bearers carry a sedan chair very much like the one in which Miss Mattie was a passenger on the night when she drew its window curtains to shut out a threatened encounter with the ghost of "a lady all in white and without her head" in Darkness Lane.

Around Knutsford there are plenty of interesting places to

visit, some of which have associations with Mrs. Gaskell. To the south are **Toft Hall,** an ancient house whose origins date back to the twelfth century, and the villages of **Lower Peover** and **Over Peover** (which has an Elizabethan hall and a fourteenth-century church where Mrs. Gaskell's parents were married).

To the north, about two miles from the center of Knutsford, is **Tatton Park,** a fine Georgian mansion designed by Samuel and Lewis Wyatt. Once the home of the Egerton family, it is now a National Trust property and contains collections of furniture, china, and silver as well as paintings by Murillo, Van Dyck, and Canaletto. The house is open to the public, along with its vast park of more than two thousand acres containing extensive woodlands, a Japanese garden, a Shinto temple, and a mere that may be one of the "ponds" they proposed to drag when Miss Mattie's runaway brother Peter disappeared (he turned up later in India). Tatton Park appears as Cumnor Towers in Mrs. Gaskell's longest and finest novel, *Wives and Daughters,* which she left unfinished at her death in 1865.

Mrs. Gaskell is buried with her husband and two of their daughters in Knutsford, at the ivy-covered **Brook Street Chapel,** where she worshiped and taught in the Sunday School.

Knutsford is still as she described it in *Cranford.* "The houses are anything but regular . . . but altogether they look well . . . here and there, a dwelling-house has a court in front, with a grass plot on each side of the flagged walk, and a large tree or two—limes and chestnuts—which send their great projecting upper branches over into the street. . . ."

LANGHARNE   (Glamorgan West): off A40, 3 mi. S of St. Clears

Dylan Thomas is said to have spent the happiest years of his turbulent life in the beautiful and remote Welsh town of Langharne, where he lies buried in the churchyard of **St. Martin's.**

Under Milk Wood, the play for voices he left incomplete, is supposedly the result of his ironic, cruel, and sometimes deeply compassionate observation of life in Langharne itself. The medieval castle dominating the shoreline is his "castle brown as owls." And when the Second Voice says, "tall as the town clocktower," it is the white tower of the old Town Hall that he meant. The characters in all their complexities are the people he saw beneath the surface. At the time the play was first broadcast, Langharne's residents were startled at their identity. They had thought Dylan Thomas just another man about town.

The house he and Caitlin lived in is a white, square-built cottage perched grandly on the undercliff, overlooking the vast sweep of the Taf Estuary, a stretch of sea and grassy, windswept islands bordering on the Pendine Sands. It is known as the **Boat House,** and can be reached by taking Dylan's Walk up the hilly streets of the town. The scenery in this area is re-created in his famous "Poem in October."

LEWES   (Sussex): on 2109, the Newhaven–Seaford Road

On the grassy slopes of the Wotuh Downs, where the River Ouse winds down to the sea, stands **Asham,** a creamy, stucco-colored house with arched windows. Virginia Woolf leased it before her marriage to Leonard Woolf in 1912, and it was their country home until 1919. The house once lay in a sheep meadow dotted with great trees, but that peaceful setting has now, unfortunately, been replaced by a cement plant. Leonard Woolf described the house during their days there as "romantic, gentle, melancholy, lonely."

After her first breakdown Virginia began to spend more and more time at Asham, where there was nothing to think about but the surrounding scenery. According to local legend the house was haunted, and after hearing noises at night over a period of years, Virginia was inspired to write her well-known story "A Haunted House."

The Bloomsbury regulars—Vanessa and Clive Bell, Roger Fry, and Duncan Grant—visited Asham often on weekends. Eventually the Bells found a house within walking distance near the village of Firle, and their house too was frequented by noted London literary people. Lytton Strachey came to read aloud his biography of Florence Nightingale and his *Eminent Victorians*. Soon thereafter John Maynard Keynes also bought a house at nearby Tilton (see Rodmell).

LICHFIELD   (Staffordshire): on A38, 15 mi. N of Birmingham

Johnson Birthplace Museum: Every year, on the Saturday nearest Samuel Johnson's birthday, his admirers gather at the Market Square in Lichfield to pay tribute to his genius. His statue there casts him in a pensive mood, sitting with bent head and downcast eyes, as if exhausted from compiling his dictionary, vast tomes of which are stacked beneath his chair. Across the square his friend and biographer James Boswell stands jauntily on a pedestal. Facing Dr. Johnson is the house in which he was born and where his father, Michael Johnson, conducted his book-selling business. The dignified and attractive building has changed little externally since then. Today it houses a valuable collection of literary treasures, as well as many of Johnson's personal relics, ranging from his shoe buckles and bib holder to his *Book of Common Prayer*.

The house has been renovated to reflect the various stages of the dictionary maker's life. Though he did almost all of his literary work in London, those first twenty-eight years in Lichfield had a great effect on him. The Johnsons' book-selling business was never very successful and the family was constantly plagued by poverty. At school he often found himself flogged for inattention, and actually received most of his education by holing up in his father's loft and reading the store's fine collection of books. After a short time at Oxford where he became very depressed about his poverty, Johnson returned to Lichfield for eight years before taking off for London with David Garrick.

The curators have attempted to have the rooms of the house reflect the Johnson family lifestyle and the different periods of

the author's life. There are exhibits relating to his early education at Lichfield and Oxford, his attempt to set up a school at
Edial Hall with David Garrick, and his early attempts at writing. One room is furnished as an early eighteenth-century book-
shop to illustrate his father's trade. Another centers on the years
in London, where he went to make his living by writing. This
was probably Samuel Johnson's most difficult period, since he
had to write in order to live and to support his aging wife,
Tetty. In the showcases are some of the works written during
this arduous time: his only play, *Irene,* his biography of Richard
Savage, and the great essays in *The Rambler.*

The birth room is set up to illustrate the period in which he
achieved great fame as a writer, and the books exhibited here
represent the major achievements of those years: a first and
fourth edition of *A Dictionary of the English Language,* the
agreement between Johnson and his publisher for a new edition
of Shakespeare's plays, and a first edition of his Oriental tale,
The History of Rasselas. Also on display are some of the personal belongings he used in London. The adjoining Hay Hunter
Library, considered a center for study on Johnson, has an extensive collection of manuscripts and books.

The top floor is devoted to the last years of Johnson, Boswell,
and Garrick. The accounts of the famous tour of the highlands
which Johnson and Boswell took, and Boswell's writings on his
trip to Corsica, are on view, in addition to some memoirs of
David Garrick—who was making acting a respectable profession
while Johnson was working on his dictionary.

There are several other Johnson associations in the town.
On **Dam Street** is an antique shop which was once Dame
Oliver's School, the first school the author attended. When
Johnson was going to Oxford, Dame Oliver came to bid him
farewell and brought a present of gingerbread, saying that he
was the best scholar she ever had.

Johnson often visited **St. Michael's Church** during his early
life and on later visits when he returned with Boswell. His
father, mother, and brother Nathaniel are buried here. Johnson
was not able to return to Lichfield to attend his mother's funeral
when she died at the age of ninety in 1759, but to pay for her
funeral and a few debts she owed he wrote his famous work

Rasselas within a fortnight. Later on, as his dictionary gave him some financial security, he erected an additional stone over the family graves and wrote an eloquent epitaph in Latin for her.

There are busts of both Johnson and Garrick in the graceful triple-spired **Lichfield Cathedral** near Market Square. Johnson's well-known epitaph on Garrick's concludes: "His death eclipsed the gaiety of nations, and impoverished the publick stock of harmless pleasure."

(Johnson Birthplace Museum is open, except bank holidays, Tues.–Sat. 10–1, 2–5. June–Sept. also open Sun. 2:30–5. Nominal charge.)

LYME REGIS   (Devon): on A35, 25 mi. W of Dorchester

Jane Austen spent many summers at Lyme Regis, an idyllic resort town on the Devon coast, where farmlands dip down to meet the sea, and set her last novel, *Persuasion,* here. The site of her cottage, Wings, is up on top of the promenade overlooking the boulder seawall and present-day marina. It is marked by a memorial plaque. Behind the cottage, which remained until 1945, when it almost toppled over, was a tea garden where Jane spent many hours looking out at the sea. Just below are the steep stairs to the beach which she describes in the novel. In one scene Louisa Musgrove falls down them and has to be taken to the home of Captain Wentworth's friends to recuperate.

MAUCHLINE   (Ayr): 11 mi. from Ayr, 6 mi. from Tar-
bolton

An inn commonly associated with Burns was **Poosie Nancie's,** across the street from the home of Jean Amour, his first love and enduring wife. This haunt is still open as an inn and tearoom. Burns is presumed to have met Jean at the Green, by

Mauchline Burn, and married her at Gavin Hamilton's house adjoining the fifteenth-century tower of Mauchline Castle. Supposedly her father hemmed and hawed about giving his permission for them to marry, even though their first child was about to be born. During the time Burns was banned from her house he would prop a ladder against the wall and climb into the window. The house on **Castle Street** where the two began housekeeping in 1788 is now marked with a plaque. **Mauchline Church** was the scene of Burns's repentance on the "Cutty Stool" because of his irregular marriage to Jean. In the churchyard, the scene of "The Holy Fair," rest four of the Burnses' legitimate children and a number of his contemporaries and friends.

MELROSE (Roxburghshire): on A6091, 3 mi. SE of Galashiels

Probably the best-known of the border abbeys is **Melrose,** whose fame was established by the often-quoted lines from Sir Walter Scott's poem "The Lay of the Last Minstrel": "If thou wouldst see fair Melrose aright/ Go visit it by the pale moonlight." Melrose, also the Kennaquhair of Scott's "The Monastery," is a very pleasant town, now well-known in sporting circles for its prowess at rugby football. Scott himself supervised the repairs to the well-preserved ruin of its abbey, which was built in the twelfth century.

NETHER STOWEY (Somerset): 8 mi. NW of Bridgwater on A39

Though Coleridge spent only three years at **Coleridge Cottage,** which stands on the present-day main street of the quiet, untouched village of Nether Stowey, it has become one of England's favorite literary spots. "The Ancient Mariner," the first part of "Christabel," and "This Lime Tree Bower My

Prison" were among the poems composed here, and it was to
this cottage that there came on a summer day of 1797 "a person
on business from Porlock," thus interrupting the inspired com-
position of "Kubla Khan." When Coleridge left the cottage
after three years, the best of his poetry had been written. He
did produce some fine prose during his later years, but had he
written no more poetry after Nether Stowey he would still be
known as one of the country's finest poets.

Coleridge left Nether Stowey in 1800, and, unfortunately,
the low thatched building was much altered in the nineteenth
century. There now remain only four rooms that existed in
his day: the room to the right of the entrance, which was the
kitchen; a sitting room to the left; and two bedrooms, reached
from the end of the sitting room by a winding stair. The adjoining cottage was built sometime later, as were the several houses
that lie between the garden and the site of Poole's Tannery in
Castle Street.

He brought with him to Nether Stowey his wife, Sarah, his
infant son, his brilliant but ill-starred brother, Hartley, a maid-
servant, Nanny, and his friend Charles Lloyd, a chronically
neurotic and ill-tempered person who caused quarrels between
his host and such notable friends as Charles Lamb. Coleridge
spoke of his pleasure with the cottage and wrote that there was
a comfortable sitting room for Lloyd, a room for the family,
another room for Nanny, a kitchen, and an outhouse. Outside, a
clear brook of "soft water" ran before the front door, a pretty
garden provided them with vegetables, and an orchard gave
them fruit.

Coleridge was also very taken by the surrounding area. During a walk with Wordsworth to nearby Dulverton the idea
underlying "The Ancient Mariner" was born, and, apart from
the direct references to places in the neighborhood, the whole
poem seems imbued with the spirit of the west country. The
Mariner sailed from Watchet, and the ship dropped below the
church of St. Decuman, which stands upon a hill on the outskirts of the town. The bluff at Minehead is thought to be the
Hermit's dwelling "in that wood which slopes down to the
sea," for the pilot came alongside here, and in those days Mine-

head would be the most likely spot for a ship making her way to Watchet to pick up her pilot.

For a short time the cottage was a gathering place for the poet's literary companions. In July, 1797, William and Dorothy Wordsworth settled at Alfoxden outside the neighboring village of Holford. Coleridge wrote that Wordsworth was an invaluable addition to the neighborhood and that he revered him as a poet, philosopher, and human being. Unfortunately, the rest of the community did not share this view and the Wordsworths left at the end of the year. Somehow the coterie at the cottage was looked at with suspicion, and the government sent an agent down to inquire into their activities. At that time England was engaged in her struggle with Napoleon and the authorities were very much concerned with quelling any suspected disaffection at home.

(Coleridge Cottage is open Easter–end Sept., 2–6. Nominal fee.)

NEWSTEAD (Nottinghamshire): 4 1/2 mi. S of Mansfield, off A60

In May, 1798, George Gordon Byron, ten years of age, inherited the heavily mortgaged and badly decayed **Newstead Abbey,** and thus became the sixth Byron baronet of the estate. Though he lived there very intermittently, mostly during his Cambridge years, he was deeply attached to the property and frequently praised it in his poetry. There is an especially nostalgic description of the abbey in the thirteenth canto of *Don Juan.*

Byron could do little to repair, much less maintain, Newstead Abbey when he finally became of age and secured the property. He came here often for parties with his friends from Cambridge, and a tradition has grown up about the excesses they indulged in. It seems they used the empty dining room as a shooting gallery for pistol practice, and at times had wild drinking parties while dressed up in monks' clothing. Byron at one point found an old monk's skull on the grounds, and had it mounted in silver and made into a drinking cup. He supposedly presented the cup at a dinner attended by many ladies of the area. No sooner had he filled the cup with wine than the figure of a headless monk appeared at the doorway, causing many of his guests to faint.

Boatswain's monument, the tomb of his dog which he carefully placed on the exact spot of the high altar, is perhaps symbolic of the youthful Byron's impudence. He picked the most sacred grounds of the ruins for the octagonal monument, topped by a Grecian urn, to celebrate the death of his beloved dog. At the time he planned to be buried there himself, along with his faithful servant Joe Murrey. Byron, however, who died in Missolonghi helping the Greeks fight for independence, was brought back and buried in the family vault in Hucknall Torkard, eight miles away; and Murrey chose to be buried elsewhere.

Contrary to popular belief, Newstead was never an abbey. Its correct name is the Priory of Saint Mary at Newstead, and according to legend it was founded by Henry II in 1170 as an act of remorse for the murder of Thomas à Becket. The priory continued as a religious community until 1539, when it was repressed as part of the English Reformation. Soon thereafter the property came into the hands of Sir John Byron of Colwick and it remained in the family until the poet Lord Byron inherited it. Legend has it that they were an eccentric family, at times prone to madness. The poet's grandfather William lives in history as "the wicked lord" or "Devil Byron," who was brought to trial in the House of Lords for the murder of his neighbor and relation William Chaworth. The poet's father, "Mad Jack Byron," created a scandal by eloping with a wealthy married woman to Paris. Unfortunately for Mad Jack, his wife died soon after the birth of their daughter, Augusta (his son, the poet, later had a child by this half-sister), and he was left without an income to support either Newstead or the baby. He soon returned to England to find another rich heiress, Catherine Gordon, who gave birth to the poet George Gordon Byron. Mad Jack deserted his wife and son soon after the birth, a pattern which was to be seen in the next generation as Lord Byron fathered children and took off soon thereafter. A very interesting

letter explaining how he loathed the upcoming birth of his
child by Annabella Milbanke is on display in the Salon.

Little of the priory remains except the crypt and cloisters,
since much of its decaying stonework was used in adapting the
buildings as a private mansion, a conversion which was accomplished in two stages—immediately after the first Byron bought
Newstead, in the 1500's, and in the 1820's, after Lord Byron
the poet had sold it. The break between priory and mansion is
quite evident in the front of the building. The crypt and
cloisters now contain relics of the abbey's nineteenth-century
owners, the Webb family. Adjoining these is the Plantagenet
Room, filled with pictures, plans, documents, and relics illustrating the history of Newstead during monastic times and the
development of the building since its purchase by the Byron
family.

Various rooms throughout the mansion contain Byron furniture. The North and East galleries, for example, contain pieces
that were until recently in private collections. Off these rooms
are the various royal bedrooms where such notables as Charles
II, Edward III, and Henry VII stayed. The Charles II Room
contains letters written by Lord Byron when he was at Cambridge. They were written to the Pigot family, to whom he was
close, and throw valuable light on his first two books of poetry.

The Salon, in monastic times the canons' refectory, in the
mansion's time the great drawing room, now houses the extensive Roe-Byron collection of Byron manuscripts, first editions, pictures, and relics, all of which are displayed in the many
showcases lined up along the Salon walls. Above the showcases
are many portraits of the Byron family, among them the famous portrait of Byron by Thomas Phillips.

Byron's bedroom, up the spiral staircase from the West
Gallery, contains the original furniture, including the elaborate
four-poster bed with gilt coronets which he took with him to
his schoolrooms at Cambridge. Also here is the table on which
he wrote *English Bards and Scotch Reviewers*.

Newstead and its many acres of beautifully manicured gardens, ponds, and forests were certainly not so immaculately
maintained during Byron's time. One of his grandfathers was
even forced to die in the scullery, since that was the only room

in the mansion with a dry roof. Since 1930 Newstead has been kept by the Corporation of Nottingham and is used by area residents as a country park.

(Newstead Abbey open Good Fri.–Sept., with tours at 2, 3, 4, 5 for nominal charge. Grounds open all year for nominal charge.)

NORTH LEES HALL (Derbyshire): 12 mi. W of Sheffield, off A625, near Hathersage

North Lees Hall, now a country guesthouse out on the open moorlands of the Peak District, is one of the houses that claims to be the Thornfield Hall of Charlotte Brontë's *Jane Eyre.* Here Mr. Rochester lived with his maniac wife closeted away on the third floor.

The original plaster friezes and ceilings, and the spiral staircase, of this gaunt fifteenth-century structure have been restored as Charlotte Brontë would have known them. The house is open to view by advance arrangement with the proprietor.

NUNEATON   (Warwickshire): 5 mi. N of Coventry on A444

Nuneaton is the center of George Eliot country. Though the area has been greatly urbanized since her time, many places of her works, especially the novel *The Mill on the Floss,* still stand and can easily be found in the town and its environs. This novel, *Adam Bede,* and *Middlemarch* all contain detailed descriptions of the surrounding Midlands countryside during her childhood.

About two miles from the town center, on the right corner of the main Nuneaton-to-Coventry Road and Arbury Lane, stands **Griff House,** the home of Mary Ann Evans for twenty-one years. Secluded by elm and chestnut trees, the exterior of the building, now a middle-priced hotel, and the grounds are as she knew them. The childhood of Maggie and Thom Tulliver of Dorlcote Mill in *The Mill on the Floss,* largely created from the childhood of the author and her brother, Isaac Pearson Evans, who also lived there, was partly set in this "trimly-kept, comfortable dwelling house as old as the elms and chestnuts that shelter it," with its "great attic that ran under the old high-pitched roof." As she described it, "This attic was Maggie's favorite retreat on a wet day, when the weather was not too cold; here she fretted out all her ill humours, and talked aloud to the worm-eaten floors and the worm-eaten shelves and the dark rafters festooned with cobwebs. . . ."

The large garden at the rear of Griff House is thought to have been the original of the Hall Farm Garden of *Adam Bede,* while the garden walk which led to the summer house is part of Lowick Manor, home of Dorothea and her husband, the Rev. Edward Casaubon, in *Middlemarch.* Immediately to the right of Griff House in the rear corner of the field is the original of the Round Pool of *The Mill on the Floss,* in which Maggie and Tom used to fish. "No one knew how deep it was; and mysterious too, that it should be almost a perfect round. . . ."

While Mary Ann was growing up here, her mother, the daughter of a yeoman farmer, energetically supervised the busy household and gardens of Griff House. She made large quantities of butter, cheese, and preserves, and was often at work at the spinning wheel. After her death, Mary Ann left school and took over the management of the house very successfully, while continuing her studies of modern and ancient languages and music. Later, before leaving to spend the rest of her life in London, she became involved in a movement to alleviate social ailments and organized clubs to help the poor, sick, and elderly.

Gipsy Lane, which joins the Nuneaton-to-Coventry Road on the Nuneaton side of the railway bridge near Griff House and continues to Bulkington Lane, had black tents pitched on both sides of its wide grass verges during the author's time. Maggie ran away to the gypsies in *The Mill on the Floss* after she had pushed "pretty little Lucy" into the mud of the pond a field away from the garden at Garum Firs, the place in the novel used to depict **Marston Hall,** Bulkington. The author often visited the house, since her aunt and uncle, a well-known gentle-

man farmer, lived there. They were the originals of Mr. and
Mrs. Pullet of that same novel.

Arbury Mill, nearly a mile from Griff House, after turning
right on the Nuneaton-to-Coventry Road, was the mill George
Eliot knew best in her childhood. Probably then, as today, the
right-hand side of the lane to Arbury Mill was bordered by a
stream, with undergrowth and woodland in the background.
Much of the description of the scenery around the full stream
as seen from the bridge in Chapter I of the novel is true of
Arbury Mill today, although the interior and exterior of Mill
House have greatly changed. The original stone stairs of the
house, on which the author supposedly sat to read and write,
are still there. The mill itself, now silent, is on the opposite
side of the lawn, and some of the old grinding wheels are still
there.

This was the mill that produced the flour of "many a good
loaf of Arbury Wheat." In the novel, however, Dorlcote Mill
was placed on the Ripple, the tributary of the Floss that is at
the spot where the actual River Idle flows into the River Trent
in Gainsborough (Lincolnshire)—her St. Oggs. For the flood
scene at the end of her story she needed a tidal river, and thus
used the Trent (the Floss) in the Gainsborough area because
of its history of catastrophic floods. At the end of the novel all
her scenes and characters were moved from the Nuneaton countryside to the Gainsborough area so that she would have the
tidal river.

Red Deeps is the name given to the part of Griff Hollows
lying between Coventry Road and the point where the Griff
Arm of the Coventry Canal joins the main canal. It is on the
left-hand side of Griff Hollows as you go to Coventry from
Nuneaton. Chapter V of the novel includes descriptions of this
beauty spot. This was the scene of meetings between Maggie
Tulliver and Philip Wakem.

Three miles southwest of the center of Nuneaton is **Arbury
Hall,** the Cheveral Manor which figures so predominantly in
her novels. The benevolent and cultivated Sir Christopher
Cheveral was in actuality Sir Roger Newdigate, its owner. Her
"Mr. Gilfil's Love-Story," in which she describes how Sir Chris-
topher transformed Cheveral Manor from ugliness into beauty,

is derived entirely from Sir Roger Newdigate's transformation
of Arbury from an Elizabethan house into a Gothic one in the
second half of the eighteenth century. By the time Eliot was
writing the rebuilding was still very much alive in the minds
of those who had witnessed it, and she was in constant contact
with those people. Her father had for many years been the
farmer, surveyor, and land agent for the South Farm on the
Arbury estate, and she, in fact, was born there. Her father is
the original of Adam Bede, Caleb Garth, and Mr. Hackit, while
her mother was portrayed in the capable, witty Mrs. Poyser of
Adam Bede and the kindly Mrs. Hackit of *Scenes of Clerical
Life*. Sister Christiana became Celia of *Middlemarch* and Lucy
Deane of *The Mill on The Floss*.

OLNEY (Buckinghamshire): 5 mi. N of Newport Pagnell on A509

Olney is a quiet market town which has two claims to fame
—the curious old custom of the Shrove Tuesday Pancake Race
and the town's associations with the poet William Cowper.
From 1767 to 1786 Cowper lived at Orchard Side, the red-
brick house that is now the **Cowper Memorial Museum,** and
many of his famous works, including *The Task* and *John
Gilpin,* were written here. Within a stone's throw of the garden
lies the vicarage where the stern Rev. John Newton, coauthor
with Cowper of the *Olney Hymns,* lived.

Cowper came here with the family of the widowed Mary
Unwin, who had taken him in after he was treated for insanity
at a St. Albans asylum, and who was a patient and loving companion to him for many years. He did continue to have frequent periods of depression during his stay here, and one
especially long one in 1773, but for the most part his years at
Olney were calm and productive. After the acute depression in
January, 1773, he experienced what he explained as a dream of
God's explicit reprobation, which was thereafter a lurking ob-
session on his mind. Although he attributed this vision to his
failure to obey a divine command to commit suicide, biog-

raphers have equated the fatal dream with a belief in pre-destination so apparent in his poems and songs. During his many fruitful years at Olney, he produced volumes of letters, translations from the Italian, Latin, and Greek, as well as such famous poems as *The Task,* which reflected his patriotism, social concern, and fervid joy in nature.

The interior of the house remains much as it was in Cowper's day, and contains many of his personal possessions. In all the rooms the walls have been lined with portraits of his friends and with pictures of places close to him. The most important displays of personal relics can be seen in the parlor cabinets. There are the Cowper family Bible, Cromwell's seal, and Cowper's snuffboxes. Many of the other display cases house archaeological exhibits of local interest and tools connected with the lacemaking industry at Olney. Perhaps the most personal touch remaining is the small casement at the back of the hall, through which he used to lure his pet hares in for their evening play periods on the carpet. These animals were often celebrated in his poetry. The Cowper family tree, dating from 1467, original drafts of the poems "To Mary" and "Yardley Oak" and a large collection of Cowper manuscripts can be seen upon request; there is also an extensive library of books on both Cowper and Newton.

The yard at the back was very important to both of them. They used to walk back and forth over what was then an orchard between the house and the vicarage. In order to do this they had a doorway built through the vicarage garden wall. For the privilege of passing through the orchard they paid a guinea a year, hence it is known as Guinea Field. At the far end of the yard, beyond the extensive garden and gravel path sixty yards long, is the Summer House, which Cowper sometimes called his boudoir or sulking room.

The path which he used to visit the gardens of another friend was frequently described in his nature poems, and especially in *The Task,* which, incidentally, Robert Burns admired greatly and carried in his pocket. This path is generally one which rises from a close called the Pigtle on the west side of Olney and is parallel to the road leading from Olney to Weston. Cowper described the "slow winding Ouse," the square tower of Clifton

Church, and the "graves, heaths, and smoking villages remote."

The nearby **Olney Parish Church,** where Newton preached and Cowper worshiped, and where so many of the Olney hymns were sung, is well worth a visit. Newton's pulpit remains as a relic in the church and his tomb is in the northeast corner of the churchyard. Of special note is a window in the Memorial Chapel of the North Aisle. Its lower portion portrays the figures of Newton and Cowper, Cowper's pet hares, and other scenes of local interest.

(Cowper Memorial Museum open Easter–Oct., Tues.–Sat. 10–12, 2–5; Nov.–Easter 2:30–4:30. Nominal charge.)

OXFORD   (Oxfordshire): 50 mi. NW of London

So many literary greats have been connected with Oxford that the university does not have many plaques commemorating them. **Balliol** alone has had the seventeenth-century essayist John Evelyn, the economist Adam Smith, and two leading poets of the nineteenth century, Matthew Arnold and A. C. Swinburne.

Trinity College next door is the alma mater of Thackeray and a long list of poets, among them Byron, Dryden, Tennyson, and Housman. Byron is remembered here for the entourage he brought—his elaborate four-poster bed, which is on view still at Newstead Abbey, his dog, and his servant—and for the wild drinking parties he held both here and at Newstead Abbey (see entry). It is said that he didn't open a book at all during his four years here.

His contemporary Shelley was perhaps more of a student at **University College,** but found himself expelled after he and his friend Hogg published a pamphlet, "The Necessity of Atheism." A very lifelike marble sculpture of him, with the muse of poetry mourning underneath, is contained in a special domed chamber built by the college after his death.

Up High Street from University College is Oxford's largest college, **Christ Church,** where Charles Lutwidge Dodgson, alias

Lewis Carroll, was a mathematics don. One summer afternoon Dodgson accompanied the dean's three daughters on a boat trip up the Thames and amused them with the fairy tale of "Alice's Adventures Underground." He later wrote out and illustrated the tale as *Alice in Wonderland.*

Opposite Christ Church is **Pembroke College,** where Samuel Johnson spent a year in 1718. He occupied a small room above the gateway. Johnson was so beset by poverty that he frequently isolated himself in his room for lack of proper clothing. According to legend, at one point he could not afford to replace his badly worn-out shoes, through which his feet and toes showed. One morning he found that some generous person had placed a new pair at his door. Overcome by pride, he threw the gift away and soon thereafter returned to his hometown of Lichfield. Johnson was said to have been as much a rebel against authority here as he was at his grammar school, where he was often flogged for inattention; however, the quality of his work so impressed his tutors that they were willing to put up with him. Decades later, in the year his *A Dictionary of the English Language* was published, the university gave him an honorary degree.

PENSHURST   (Kent): 5 mi. SW of Tonbridge

Sir Philip Sidney is thought to have described his childhood home of **Penshurst Place** in the sylvan paradise of *Arcadia.* The estate is a classical medieval manor, standing close to the village but secluded from it. In fact, the only place where the house, village, and parish church can be viewed together is on the road approaching from the southeast as it crosses the River Medway. The main structure is basically a medieval manor house which has sixteenth- and nineteenth-century additions; it houses an important collection of seventeenth- and eighteenth-century furniture. The gardens, however, have been re-created in the original Elizabethan design.

The great hall of Penshurst, probably the least altered medieval hall surviving in England, forms the center of the manor house. The unusual roof, designed by the king's carpenter in 1385, consists of a system of chestnut posts, supporting beams, and enormous arched braces held up by carved figures. Above the hearth a still-blackened porthole survives to show where the smoke once rose to the roof. Originally it probably left through an open hole; this was covered over by tin in the nineteenth century when the roof was closed in. Traces of wall paintings of men-at-arms standing beneath Gothic canopies can be seen between the windows.

The undercroft and state dining room have not been altered by the redecoration of later centuries, and they have retained their basic medieval look. Part of the undercroft was cut off to make a wine cellar, but the remaining section has been decorated with suits of armor and military paraphernalia. The halls and walls immediately before the state dining room are also very medieval, with coarse stone and arched doorways. The dining room itself has the medieval walls, arched doorways, and fireplaces of smooth stone. Though furnished in mid-nineteenth-century style, the walls were not covered with eighteenth-century wall paneling and the room still has the beamed ceilings and spaciousness of a few centuries ago.

The staterooms at Penshurst do not have such a medieval aura. They are magnificently decorated with appliqué wall hangings, lacquered and gilt furnishings brought from France and Italy, and elaborate chandeliers—quite far removed from the tranquil Arcadia. Throughout the rooms are various paintings belonging to the generations of Sidneys who have lived here.

But the gardens are certainly most important in terms of literary associations since they are so inspiring. Documentary evidence suggests that the layout of the gardens took place during Philip Sidney's later years, when he was not actually in residence here. During his youth most of the area was the idyllic wood described in *Arcadia*, with a few wild gardens here and there, similar to places described outside Rome and Athens. It was Philip's father, Sir Henry Sidney, who leveled ground to make the great pond and brought over many fruit trees from the Continent. Penshurst became famous for its fruit and was praised in a poem written by Ben Jonson: "The garden flowers fresh as the air, and new as . . . the house . . . hang on the walls that every child may reach."

The garden, laid out on a rigid geometrical plan, is divided into four quarters by the drive and great walk leading past the front of the house to Diana's Bath. Conceived as a series of enclosed spaces, each part of the gardens is shut off from the view of the next, and surrounded either by walls or hedges of yew. However, some of the rigid formality is now lost and you can see from garden to garden while walking around.

(Penshurst Place is open irregularly in spring; July–end Sept., Tues., Wed., Thurs., Sat., Sun. 1–6. Admission charged.)

PORTSMOUTH (Hampshire)

Dickens Birthplace Museum: Dickens is thought to have been writing of his early childhood in Portsmouth through the character of David Copperfield. As David "looked back to the blank of his infancy," he remembered his young nurse watching him from a low kitchen window as he trotted about in the back-yard with his little sister, Fanny, and the chickens. The house of the novel is almost identical to this red-brick Georgian house at 39e Commercial Road, where Dickens lived until the age of four months, and to another on Hawkes Street, destroyed in the Blitz, where he lived until age two, when the family left for London. Both were city row houses with a small garden in front and a chicken yard in the back.

It is interesting to see Dickens' simple beginnings. Such a contrast to the elaborate houses he had later in life after he had established himself as a writer! His father, John, was not so fortunate. Often living way beyond his means, he was constantly running from the bill collectors. During the time the family lived at the birthplace house Mrs. Dickens' father, the author's grandfather, misappropriated sums of money for which he was responsible in the Navy Pay Office and hurriedly left the country. With his departure went the subsidy he was giving his son and daughter-in-law, Charles Dickens' parents, and the family was forced to move to the more modest house on Hawke Street, and two years later to London, where John Dickens ended up in debtors' prison.

When the city of Portsmouth took over the house in 1903 it was barely intact, the basement kitchen-parlor completely filled with rubble. It has since been restored to a small, modest town house, illustrating the atmosphere into which Charles Dickens was probably born. Although there are no original furnishings except for the built-in kitchen cabinet, the interior has been decorated to reflect the style in which the family probably lived during their short stay here. The most prized possession in the house is the couch on which Dickens died on June 9, 1870. This and the ornate dressing table beside it were brought from his last home at Gad's Hill, Kent.

Portraits of the novelist are hung in every room, and there are many examples of his signature at various periods of his life. Also on display are his birth, marriage, and death certificates, and the record of his christening at Kingston Church, Portsmouth. The church was demolished, but the font is now at the Church of St. Alban in Copnor, an adjoining suburb. Other documents include his life insurance, many private letters, checks, and small personal effects. On the copy of his will here he states that he does not want to be the subject of any monument or testimonial whatever, but rather wants to be remembered for his published works. For this reason, no statue of Charles Dickens exists in Britain. One exhibit centers around his works, with first editions and drawings, sketches, and paintings of the most famous characters and scenes from the novels, and another around his lifelong interest in the theater. The Portsmouth Theatre Royal, an important setting in *Nicholas Nickleby,* no longer survives, but there are a number of theatrical notices and playbills from the theater here.

(Dickens Birthplace Museum is open all year, daily 10–5. Nominal charge.)

ROCHESTER   (Kent): 25 mi. E of London

No town but London appears so frequently in Dickens' work. He became acquainted with Rochester as a child while living in the adjacent village of Chatham and stored up many impressions of the town's quaint old houses, cathedral, and ancient castle overlooking the Medway. Rochester appears under its own name in *Pickwick Papers* and *David Copperfield* and in many other works as Mudfog or Dudborough Town. In *A Christmas Carol* he described Rochester as "a little market town . . . with its bridge, its church, and widening river."

Just beyond the bridge where Mr. Pickwick used to stand and muse over the view of the Medway is the **Victoria and Bull,** an old coaching inn with colonnaded yard and handsome winding staircase, where Queen Victoria once slept. It is the historic Bull of *Pickwick Papers,* which Mr. Jingel recommended to Moses Pickwick as a "good house with nice beds," and still has the old ballroom with glass chandeliers and "elevated den" where the musicians played. Mr. Pickwick's room, No. 17, was supposedly used by Dickens and contains some of his furniture from Gad's Hill Place. In *Great Expectations* this inn was the Blue Boar, where a celebration was held in honor of Pip's being bound apprentice to Joe Gargery. His sister, so excited by the twenty-five guineas Miss Havisham had provided for the premium, proclaimed that nothing but dinner at the Blue Boar would be suitable for the occasion. So, far into the night Pumblechook, the Hubbles, and Mr. Wopsle celebrated. Several modern additions have also taken Dickens nomenclature. There is the Modern Pickwick Restaurant and The Great Expectations Bar, both in the back courtyard.

Just opposite the inn is the **Town Hall** where Pip's apprenticeship was made official. Then on down High Street, away from the bridge and opposite the old King's Inn, is **College Gate,** the Jasper's Gate of *Mystery of Edwin Drood,* with a plaque in Dickens' honor on its right side. It is one of the three surviving entrances to the cathedral grounds, which figure very strongly in the background description of *Edwin Drood,* and are also mentioned in *Great Expectations* and *Pickwick Papers*.

Farther down, on the opposite side of the street, stands **Eastgate House,** with its high gables, old beams, and timbers, which was the young ladies' seminary by the same name in *Edwin Drood*. Here Miss Twinkleton presided and Rosa Bud received her education. The house is now a museum of local relics containing furniture, guns, antique fire engines, and models of the city in earlier times. Near the entrance is a display case of Dickens memorabilia containing his walking stick and paperweight. In the back garden of the house is Dickens' Swiss Chalet, the outdoor study in which he worked on the grounds of his mansion at Gad's Hill.

Up on Maidstone Road is **Restoration House,** the Satis House of *Great Expectations,* where the "immensely rich and grim lady" Miss Havisham lived amid the ruins of her wedding. The house takes its name from an overnight visit Charles II made while traveling from Dover to London on May 28, 1660, the night of the Restoration. A series of large tapestries which the monarch donated to the house are still preserved. The dark, moss-covered structure remains as Dickens described it, "a large and grim house barricaded against the robbers."

(Eastgate House is open daily except Fri. 2–5:30; closed Dec. 25, 26. Free. Restoration House is open by appointment only for a small entry fee.)

ROCKINGHAM   (Northamptonshire): 6 mi. N of Uppingham on A6003

Rockingham Castle, a favorite Dickens haunt, is a classic country fortress. During the Middle Ages it was used by the English kings as an administrative center in the Midlands and as a hunting lodge, since Northamptonshire offered the best sport in the country. By the sixteenth century, when royalty was decorating the castles of the south with great art and lavish embellishments, Rockingham was leased by a local landowner and converted into a Tudor family home. Though it has the appearance of a medieval stronghold, with its keep, portcullis, moat, and many outbuildings, the interior reflects a simpler living style and is without the great staterooms which were often dedicated to castles by visiting royalty.

Dickens wrote part of *Bleak House* while he was a guest here, and the Chesney Wold of that novel is believed to be patterned after Rockingham. He himself wrote that he had "taken many bits, chiefly about trees and shadows, from observations made at Rockingham." There are striking similarities between this setting and his description of Sir Leicester Dedlock's Lincolnshire mansion, Chesney Wold. Rockingham stands on the top of a hill overlooking the Welland River valley, very similar to the marshy landscape around Chesney Wold. The castle's Yew Walk is almost identical to the Ghost's Walk at Sir Dedlock's garden, and both places have sundials. Chesney Wold's interior also resembles Rockingham. Even the surrounding village is similar. One street leads up the hill from the village of Rockingham to the castle. On it is a small country inn called Sondes Arms, which could very well have been the prototype for Dedlock Arms in the novel.

Dickens is vividly remembered at Rockingham. A number of relics associated with him are on display in the Billiard Room. There are copies of his letters to the Watsons, his hosts, the copy of *David Copperfield* he presented to them, and the original playbills of the amateur theatricals in which Dickens, both as actor and storyteller, took part while he was a guest at the castle in 1851.

The scene of the performances was the Long Gallery, which occupies the upper floor of the completely new wing built in 1553—an immense and beautiful apartment which was illustrated in early editions of *Bleak House*.

(Rockingham Castle is open Easter–end Sept., Thurs., Sun., and bank holidays 2–6. Admission charged.)

RODMELL   (Sussex): 5 mi. E of Brighton

In 1919 Virginia and Leonard Woolf came here to **Monk's House**, which was to be their country home for the next twenty-two years. In writing about their marriage Leonard told of the tranquil effect Monk's House had on Virginia and how it perhaps enabled her to carry on as long as she did.

Rodmell has changed little since the Woolfs' time. From the ancient Rodmell Church you can look over the wall to get a glimpse of Monk's House, which stands amid a labyrinth of foliage and flowers. Virginia wrote of the foxes and pheasants they often saw as she and Leonard walked around the village.

On March 28, 1941, Virginia left Monk's House for the last time. She had completed *Between the Acts* and once again felt madness approaching. After writing letters to her sister, Vanessa, and to Leonard, she put a large stone into her pocket and walked into the River Ouse. Leonard died there twenty-eight years later, at the age of eighty-eight.

RUGBY   (Warwickshire): 10 mi. E. of Coventry on A428

Rugby School was the setting for *Tom Brown's School Days,* the autobiographical novel by Thomas Hughes which documented life at a typical English public school. Featured in the novel was Thomas Arnold, "the Doctor" (as he was known to Tom Brown), who virtually founded the English public-school system as it exists today—with a system of democratic discipline imposed by students themselves, from prefects and senior boys downward through the school.

The present buildings of Rugby School date from the nineteenth century and form an impressive group with the Close and the green turf of the playing fields alongside. Several other famous writers besides Thomas Hughes were educated here— Lewis Carroll and the poets Matthew Arnold and Rupert Brooke. Matthew Arnold's poem "Rugby Chapel" referred to the predecessor of the present chapel, which was erected in 1872. It has a fine east window containing sixteenth-century glass. The museum also has many items of interest, including the hand of the clock that, in the book, Tom Brown and his friend managed to climb on and scratch their names. And gazing thoughtfully across the Close is a statue of Thomas Hughes.

RYDAL   (Cumbria): 2 mi. N of Ambleside

Wordsworth came to **Rydal Mount** in 1813 with his wife, their three children, his sister, Dorothy, and sister-in-law Sara Hutchinson, after having lived a few miles away at Dove Cottage in Grasmere and for a short time at Allenbank. His new position as exciseman for Westmoreland County enabled him to live out his life here in modest comfort. By the time he came here, however, his best works had already been written. Except for a revision of *The Prelude* and some minor poems, his period of great genius was behind him. The Dove Cottage years, especially during the time when he was associated with Coleridge, had been his most prolific.

This house, like Dove Cottage, continued to be a gathering place for Lake District poets, novelists, and scholars. Dorothy Wordsworth wrote that the children of Coleridge, Southey, and Matthew Arnold also enjoyed romping around the spacious grounds at Rydal Mount. William continued to be a devoted gardener, designing not only the four-and-a-half acres of garden on his own property but also many gardens for friends and neighbors. He believed that a garden should be informal, harmonize with the countryside, and consist of "lawn and trees carefully planted so as not to obscure the view." Though the property is now slightly overgrown, the gardens have that wild yet controlled aura that is very much Wordsworth.

The house contains many pieces of furniture that had been in the hands of various family members since Wordsworth's death, and a number of family portraits that were there during his time. The dining room, with its old oak beams and original slate floor, has the original needlepoint seats that Dorothy and Mary Wordsworth worked on. At the far end of this room is a copy of the famous Hayden portrait of the poet. Here also are smaller pictures of family members and Lakeland views.

Wordsworth's small library here contains the only known portrait of his sister, Dorothy, and also the famous Inman portrait of Coleridge. A servant at Rydal Mount once aptly mentioned to a visitor, "This is my master's library where he keeps his books; his study is out of doors." In 1968 the study, or library, and the drawing room were made into one room. The drawing room at Rydal Mount was the scene of many festive occasions. Wordsworth once wrote that in this room, where he did a lot of dictating, there had just been a dance with "forty Beaus and Belles besides Matrons, Spinsters and Greybeards" and that on the next day they were to have a venison feast.

In William and Mary's bedroom are the portraits of Queen Victoria and the Prince of Wales that were presented to him when he became poet laureate. The view from the window overlooks Dora's field and Rydal Chapel. Wordsworth bought the field—at a time when he thought he might be turned out of the house—and intended to build on it. After differences with his landlady the field became the garden of his favorite daughter, Dora, who came home to die at Rydal Mount in 1847 after five years in Portugal with her young husband.

Wordsworth's upstairs study, probably added to the house around 1838, contains a valuable collection of first editions, and also a few personal possessions. The ceiling is a copy of one that he admired in Italy, on his second tour of the Continent.

(Rydal Mount is open Mar.–Dec., 10–12:30 and 2–5:30 daily. Small entry fee.)

RYE   (Sussex): 10 mi. NE of Hastings

Lamb House, which towers over steep, cobbled West Street, had long been thought the Mansion House of Rye when Henry James came here to live in 1897. For several hundred years it had been occupied by the Grebell and Lamb families, who held the mayoralty of Rye over a long period.

James wrote much about the house during his early tenancy. He was especially enchanted by the garden's banqueting chamber, which he used as a study. There he spent his mornings dictating novels and stories to his secretary, who recorded them directly on the "Remington Machine." It is said that the long, involved sentences of his later novels reflect this method of writing.

Many of his best-known novels were written here—*The Am-
bassadors, The Golden Bowl,* and *The Wings of the Dove.*
During his first few months at Lamb House he wrote an autobiographical novel, *The Awkward Age.* One of its main characters, Mr. Longden, who had retreated from London to the
country, was modeled on James himself, and his "old, square,
red-roofed" house was based on Lamb House.

James often entertained local residents at tea parties, and
had such celebrities as H. G. Wells and Gilbert Chesterton as
houseguests. In 1948 the James family presented Lamb House
to the National Trust, who repaired the damage done during
a 1940 bombing and set aside a small room as a memorial to him.

The old vicarage of Rye up on Market Street has become
famous as the birthplace of the playwright and poet John
Fletcher. His father was minister of the church.

(Lamb House is open Mar.–Oct., Wed. and Sat. 2–6. Nominal
charge.)

ST. IVES (Cornwall): N of A30 at SW end of Cornwall

As a child, Virginia Woolf spent her summers at a large white
house which still stands on Talland Road, overlooking the har-
bor and St. Ives Bay. From here she could see across the water
to Godrevy Lighthouse on a small island. Years later that view
came across in her novel *To the Lighthouse,* even though most
of the novel was set in Scotland.

D. H. Lawrence also lived in the area for a while, in the adjoining village of Zennor. From 1914 until 1917 the Lawrences
lived at a small stone cottage called Higher Tregarthen, and for
a time Katherine Mansfield and Middleton Murry, who had
returned to England from the French Riviera, lived with them.

Though Lawrence and his wife, Frieda, loved the countryside
of the area, they did not get on with the Cornish people, who
were suspicious of him and particularly of Frieda. World War I
had just broken out and Frieda was German. Their mail was
held and read, and their cottage often searched. Finally they

were expelled from the country. Lawrence related these experiences in his short novel *Kangaroo,* published in 1923.

SALISBURY   (Wiltshire): on A36, 20 mi. NW of Southampton

The beautiful cathedral town of Salisbury has inspired both writers and artists. It was the Barchester of the novels of Anthony Trollope and the Melchester of Thomas Hardy. Charles Dickens and Henry Fielding also referred to it, and Samuel Pepys recorded a visit here in his famous seventeenth-century diary. On canvas, John Constable, the celebrated English landscape artist, made the cathedral spire the centerpiece of a well-known picture, "Salisbury from the Meadows." More recently William Golding explored the divine madness of the bishop in *The Spire.*

In his *Autobiography,* Anthony Trollope related how in 1851 he visited Salisbury, spending many hours walking around the cathedral grounds, "and whilst wandering there one midsummer evening round the purlieus of the cathedral I conceived the story of *The Warden,* from whence came that series of novels of which Barchester, with its bishops, deans and archdeacon, was the central site."

Salisbury Cathedral has the tallest spire in England. With the exception of the 404-foot spire, the Chapter House, the west front, and the cloisters, the structure was completed in the incredibly short space of forty years. There were no major additions and so, unlike many other medieval cathedrals, it is seen today virtually as its original designers envisaged it more than 750 years ago. Christopher Wren, son of the vicar of a nearby parish and the architect of St. Paul's Cathedral, London, knew it well and described it as "one of the finest patterns of architecture of the age wherein it was built."

Just outside Salisbury, on the A30 going westward, is **Wilton House,** the palatial home of the Earls of Pembroke for over 400 years. It was built by Sir William Herbert, the first Earl of Pembroke, who was given Wilton Abbey and the surrounding lands by Henry VIII during the time he was dissolving monasteries. Wilton Abbey dated back to the eighth century, when a priory was established there by King Egbert; and during the six hundred years following it grew into a wealthy manor. Henry VIII destroyed most of those buildings and sent its thirty-one nuns fleeing to retire in a neighboring village. Today only one of the original buildings remains, the small stone court of the Belhouse.

Wilton House is certainly one of the most opulent great houses in England. Hans Holbein, the court painter and designer, was consulted for its interior, and Inigo Jones designed its elaborate seventeenth-century staterooms. The collection of art and antiques is among the best in the country. Its walls are hung with a number of Rembrandts, Rubenses, and Van Dycks, and its rooms furnished with Greek and Roman sculptures. The extensive grounds include twenty acres of lawns with giant cedars of Lebanon.

In 1575 the then Lord Pembroke married Mary Sidney, sister of the poet, and the two patronized the stage and literature, entertaining many writers at Wilton House. One historian commented that Wilton House was "like a college with so many learned persons." Ben Jonson and Edmund Spenser were among those often found there. In fact, Philip Sidney wrote *Arcadia* while visiting, and dedicated it to his sister. Scenes from that long poem are painted on all four sides of the Single Cube, one of the six staterooms. Shakespeare and his company of players are believed to have put on a performance of either *Twelfth Night* or *As You Like It* sometime around 1600, and there are a number of artifacts related to him about the house. In fact, Shakespeare dedicated his first folio of works to William, an Earl of Pembroke, and his brother, Philip.

(Wilton House is open Apr.–Oct., Tues.–Sat. and bank holidays 11–6; Sun. 2–5:30. Admission charged.)

SAWREY (Cumbria): S of Ambleside on road to Hawks-head

Anyone nurtured on Beatrix Potter's tales will enjoy a visit to **Hill Top Farm,** now a National Trust. Both house and farm are as she left it, except for the electric light on the second floor and the electric fire in the dining room.

The author and illustrator first came to Sawrey in 1896 on a summer vacation with her parents, fell in love with Hill Top, and later bought it with royalties from *The Tale of Peter Rabbit,* which began as an illustrated letter sent to the son of her former governess.

Six of her nursery classics are set at Hill Top Farm and Sawrey. The garden where Jemima Puddleduck set out in her shawl and poke bonnet in search of a secret nesting place is precisely the same today. A look up toward the house from the bottom of the garden brings the exact view illustrated in the last page of the book. Those who know *The Tale of Tom Kitten* can easily reenact the plot of that story while walking through the house. Just inside the front door is the old dresser which Aunt Maria ran past with her plate of dough, and to the back is the staircase where Tabitha Twitchit mewed for Tom.

An entire second-floor room is devoted to the author's illustrations and sketchbooks. Also on exhibit are her childhood dolls and a copy of the doll's house from *The Tale of Peter Rabbit* and *The Tale of Two Bad Mice.*

(Hill Top Farm is open Apr.–Oct., weekdays 11–5:30, Sun. 2–5:30. Small entry fee.)

SHALLOWFORD   (Staffordshire): 5 mi. NW of Stafford

Aside from the Bible and *Pilgrim's Progress,* Izaak Walton's *The Compleat Angler* is the third biggest best seller in the English language. The secret of Walton's appeal lies not so much in his angling instruction as in the peaceful serenity which pervades his work from beginning to end. The book was published when its author was sixty years old and a retired London businessman.

Walton often found contentment on the Dove River in the Midlands, and it was here that his close friend Charles Cotton lived. Cotton contributed the chapters on fly casting to the first edition of the book. After 1655, when Walton bought his retirement cottage in Shallowford, the two spent much time together, both here and at Cotton's home, Beresford Hall.

There is now a paved road right to the cottage, and a railroad runs alongside the river where Walton spent so much of his time fishing. One small room of the cottage is open as a museum of fishing equipment and Walton memorabilia sent from angling clubs around the world.

SHERWOOD FOREST (Nottinghamshire): up A60 several mi. N of Nottingham

Among the great heroes of English literature are Robin Hood and his accomplice Little John. The earliest mention of Robin yet discovered is in the second version of Langland's *Piers Plowman*, written about 1377, where the slothful priest confesses that he cannot say his paternoster perfectly, but "I can rhyme of Robin Hood." These rhymes have not survived, but from the early sixteenth century onward many ballads mentioning the notorious outlaw have come down to us. Robin Hood has been identified both as a fugitive listed in the Yorkshire pipe roll of 1230 and as a man of substance in the Yorkshire town of Wakefield a hundred years later. Both Robin Hood and Little John were praised for the same reason: they robbed from the rich to help the poor.

The ballads show Robin Hood and his men roaming over a wide stretch of country covered by the forest of Sherwood and Barnsdale, no doubt moving from one district to another when things became too hot for them. Though Sherwood Forest is

not as vast as in Robin's day, it is possible to go north from
Nottingham on A60 and pass through a number of sites associated with the legend.

At **Edwinstowe** is the church where Robin Hood is said to
have married Maid Marian. Here, too, Sherwood County Park
begins. The famous Major Oak can be reached by a broad footpath from the parking lot on the left. This tree is thirty feet in
circumference and its hollow center wide enough to hide a
dozen of Robin Hood's followers. Nearby, the Shambles Oak,
or Robin Hood's Larder, where he hung his venison, is almost
a wreck. Two interesting estates in the area are the 3,800-acre
Clumber Park and Thoresby Hall, where in the forecourt there
stands a statue of Robin Hood by Tussaud-Birt (a grandson of
Mme. Tussaud, founder of the famous wax museum).

In the town of **Blidworth,** by the side of the churchyard path,
is Will Scarlet's grave. He was one of Robin Hood's lieutenants,
and the stone marking his grave is probably the pinnacle from
the medieval church tower. In the old village yard stands a house
which is said to have been Maid Marian's home before her
marriage to Robin. King John often stayed at Blidworth Dale
when hunting in Sherwood Forest and kept his hunting dogs
at Haywood Oaks.

At **Fountaindale,** between Blidworth and Harlow Wood,
Friar Tuck's Well can be found. A bridle way now crosses the
site where the conflict between Robin and the friar is supposed
to have taken place. Sir Walter Scott wrote part of *Ivanhoe* here
and brought Robin Hood into the novel—thinly disguised as an
outlaw named Locksley—after being told of local legends.

Robin Hood's Stables at Papplewick is the name given to a
cave out in the sandstone, where he is believed to have secreted
his horses. The village church there—scene of the wedding of
Allan-a-Dale, Robin's musical comrade—contains two early-
medieval grave slabs to forest wardens, each stone carved with
bow and arrow, sling, knife, and hunting horn. And at nearby
Worksop Priory, in a cupboard near the vestry door, is a skull
with an arrowhead lodged in it. This is said to be all that remains of a forester shot by Robin Hood.

Farther on at **Hathersage,** in the Derbyshire Peak District,
Little John's grave lies in the churchyard sheltered by two yew

trees. The thirteen-foot grave is enclosed within a low-spiked iron fence. At its head is the message: "Here lies buried Little John, the friend and lieutenant of Robin Hood. He died in a cottage (now destroyed) to the east of the churchyard." In 1728 the grave was opened and a thighbone 32 inches long was found, indicating that John Little, as he was correctly named, must have been seven feet tall. His green cap is said to have hung in the church together with his longbow, which is now in Cannon Hall Museum near Barnsley, in Yorkshire.

In this area of **Barnsdale Forest,** Robin Hood and Little John met. Here, in the thirteenth century, merchants with valuables often traveled with a guard of eight to twenty archers. One day Robin Hood, at midpoint on a log-spanning stream, met a stranger taller by a head and neck and broader in shoulder by twice the breadth of Robin's hand. They fenced with quarter-staffs, and Robin was tossed into the water. Then Robin challenged the stranger with bow and arrow, and only by splitting his opponent's arrow in the target did he win. The tall stranger called himself John Little, but the outlaws nicknamed him Little John. His career would have been short indeed had not Robin Hood rescued him when he had been tied to a tree by the sheriff's men.

One winter afternoon Little John took Robin, mortally ill, to Kirklees Priory, near Brighouse, Yorkshire, to be tended by his cousin, the Prioress. Aware that he was dying, Robin blew three blasts on his horn, and Little John, awaiting his master in the forest, forced his way into the gatehouse. Though Robin shot an arrow to locate his grave site, he was buried not at the arrow's landing but at a spot about 650 yards beyond the gatehouse and 200 yards east of Highway A644.

The grave is now enclosed within a low stone wall, which bears an inscription in medieval English, with the date in Latin:

> Here underneath this little stone
> Lies Robert, Earl of Huntingdon.
> Never archer was like him so good
> And people called him Robin Hood.
> Such outlaws as he and his men
> Will England never see again.

There is much speculation as to whether this is or was the site of Robin Hood's grave. Some say that the language is not typical of the period, and others claim that the grave was excavated in the eighteenth century and nothing was found.

SISSINGHURST (Kent): 1 1/2 mi. NE of Cranbrook, off A262

Sissinghurst Castle: Sissinghurst was a great Tudor mansion fallen to shambles until 1930, when poet, novelist, and botanist Victoria Sackville-West and her statesman husband, Harold Nicolson, bought the estate, restored the surviving buildings, and built around them some of the loveliest gardens in all England. The drama of this long, tedious renovation has been recorded in their meticulous journals, in Sackville-West's many works on gardening, and in the many recent accounts of their lives and work there.

The word "castle" is misleading, since it brings tourists in search of rambling fortifications. Sissinghurst was actually built as a comfortable manor of the Middle Ages and did not acquire the title "castle" until the mid-eighteenth century, when it became a prison for French prisoners of war. During the twelfth century, a manor house stood on the spot where the orchard now lies, and it was surrounded by a moat, two sections of which still exist and are filled with water. Nothing of that house, which was graced by a visit from Edward I and his retinue in 1305, survives, but on the higher ground slightly to the west is the entrance range of the great new house that took its place. The center of that house was the present gatehouse and arch. The adjoining fifteenth-century great hall, chapel, and other buildings have long disappeared. During the sixteenth century the owner built a chapel in the orchard and installed a private chaplain in the detached sixteenth-century building still known as the Priest's House. Soon thereafter the family lost most of its fortune and Sissinghurst began to decline. When Horace Walpole visited it in 1752, he found "a park in ruins and a house in ten times greater ruins." It was at that point that the grounds were leased to the government as a prison for French seamen captured during the Seven Years' War.

The serene Sissinghurst created in the twentieth century had been one of the worst prisons during the war. Doors and windows were bricked up to prevent prisoners from escaping the overcrowding, filth, and disease. To be sent to Sissinghurst was considered the worst fate that could befall a French prisoner in English hands. Prisoners were murdered by their guards, and guards by their prisoners. In retaliation the Frenchmen broke up the house, burning for firewood the furniture of the chapel, the paneling, and even the doors and window frames. By 1800 all but the Priest's House, the tower, and the end of the south wing had been torn down. The remaining buildings were used as a parish workhouse and later as tenant farmer's quarters until 1930. Then the entire estate was rescued by Victoria Sackville-West, who had been searching Kent for a place where she could make a garden, when her new home, Long Barn near Sevenoaks, was threatened by commuters' development.

The restoration and planning of the gardens are said to reflect the nature of the marriage between Sackville-West and Nicolson, a fusion between the classical and romantic temperaments. While Harold Nicolson created the design and symmetry of the garden, his wife clothed them with plants and flowers. She made the gardens very English, very Kentish, but added a foreign touch, almost as if she were planning the garden for a Norman manor house. There were gardens for each season, and in later years she gave separate gardens their own predominant color.

The restoration of their living quarters is also interesting in light of recent biographies. There was no main house for the Nicolson family. The dining room and kitchen were in the Priest's House, Sackville-West's sitting room in the tower, Nicolson's study in the South Cottage, and the children's quarters in the long building in front.

The highlight of Sissinghurst is its tower. On the first floor is the sitting room which Sackville-West occupied from 1931 until her death in 1962. From its windows she "could see without being seen," when not wishing to be disturbed; and she would work here, often late into the night, on her many books, copies of which are shelved along with Nicolson's on a wall beneath the window. On her writing table are portraits of the Brontë sisters, Harold Nicolson, and her close friend Virginia Woolf, and some of the source books for her last biography, *Daughter of France,* published in 1960. The walls are lined with books reflecting her special interests: English literature to the right of the door, history and travel in the far left-hand corner, and gardening books on the right of the turret alcove. Beneath the west window is the couch on which she often rested. The remainder of the room is full of mementos from her many trips abroad, Sackville miniatures, and pictures and manuscripts by her friends.

On the second floor of the tower is a small museum illustrating the history of the house and the making of the garden. Its central exhibit is the printing press with which Virginia and Leonard Woolf printed the first edition of *The Waste Land,* by T. S. Eliot, and other early publications of the Hogarth Press, which they had set up in their house in Tavistock Square, London, during the early 1930's. Around the walls are photographs of the garden forty years ago and drawings of the castle as it may have appeared in earlier centuries. In the turret are diaries, letters, and manuscripts by Sackville-West and Harold Nicolson, recording their first discovery of Sissinghurst and its gradual transformation.

The top floor of the tower now contains an exhibit illustrating the work of the National Trust. From here you can see over the garden and a large part of the Kentish Weald. To the north is the long range of the North Downs, seen across the eight-mile-wide valley of the Weald. Maidstone and Canterbury are just beyond the ridge, to the north and northeast respectively. Closer are the church towers of Frittenden (north) and Biddenden (east).

The library in the tower courtyard was a dark, dirty stable until 1930, when it was transformed into a large beamed room. At that time a huge window was added at the north end and a fireplace built opposite the main door. Along two walls of the room over four thousand books are stacked from floor to ceiling. The room is furnished with family portraits, a mixture of

Italian, French, and early English furniture, and a collection of early Persian pottery.

The gardens, deserving careful perusal, can perhaps be better appreciated after you look at the exhibits in the tower: the rose garden, with a center of circular yew hedges; the spring garden; the cottage garden; and the herb garden and nuttery near the moat. At the corner, where two sides of the moat meet, is an octagonal summer house or gazebo, built in 1969 and dedicated to the memory of Harold Nicolson. This was the site of the original medieval manor house.

(Sissinghurst Castle is open Apr.–mid-Oct., Mon.–Fri. 12–6:30; Sat., Sun., and bank holidays 10–6:30. Small entry fee.)

STEVENTON (Hampshire): 5 mi. SW of Basingstoke, just N of A30

Steventon is a small secluded village with a few dozen houses scattered along one side of a winding road. All that can be seen of **Hampshire Rectory,** Jane Austen's birthplace, is its site on a meadow beside the lane leading up to the thirteenth-century church. The old pump of this house still stands there in the field and is roped off by markers. *Sense and Sensibility* and *Northanger Abbey*—both works written soon after the Austens left Steventon for Bath—reflect the isolation and romantic melancholy their author must have felt here.

STOKE POGES (Buckinghamshire): 3 mi. NE of Slough

Down a tree-lined country lane is the churchyard where Thomas Gray envisioned his immortal "Elegy in a Country Churchyard." The actual spot can be reached by walking in from the main road past the vicarage on the left and through a series of gardens, and down a rose-tree-lined path to **Stoke Poges Church.**

Gray, a professor of modern languages at Cambridge, was buried beside his mother on August 6, 1771, under the same tombstone that carries his inscription to her, "to the careful tender mother of many children, one of whom had the misfortune to survive her."

Gray's ancient yew still casts its shade on this rural churchyard, though it is now far from "neglected," and the tower of the church is no longer "ivy-mantled." The epitaph that Gray had written for his mother left no room on the stone for the addition of his own name. Instead it is inscribed on the wall of the church a few feet away. In 1799, a group of admirers, feeling that he did not have the proper memorial, erected him a huge monument with many lines from the famous poem. This can be reached by taking a footpath which diverts a little to the left into the fields on the way back to the main road.

STOKE-ON-TRENT (Staffordshire): 35 mi. NW of Birmingham

Bennett House at 205 Waterloo Road, Cobridge, served as a setting for many events in Arnold Bennett's novels of the Five Towns and is now open as a museum. Though the author left the area in his early twenties to take up residence in London, he returned to Stoke-on-Trent and his family home often to collect material for his fiction, digging up old historical records and relying on the anecdotes of friends.

The mundane existence Bennett led here comes out very clearly in his novels. Both his father and mother were devout Methodists who instilled a rigorous sense of moral duty in their children. Any child's play was considered trivial, and when not assigned to household chores the children were instructed in the Bible. Bennett found little satisfaction in the constant round of church activities; in *Clayhanger* he shows with some bitterness the excessive zeal of a young minister, probably a copy of the Rev. Appleby, who taught his Bible class on Saturday afternoons. In his late teens Bennett went the way of most proper middle-class men, making a daily trip to the nearby town of Hanley, where he collected rent for a local solicitor.

Many of his relatives were typical representatives of the potters, drapers, and small tradesmen who appear in his works. The purchase of this house, one of the many imposing villas built by those prosperous in the pottery factories, represented several generations of hard work on the part of the Bennett family. The author's father had become a solicitor after years at such mundane occupations as potter and pawnbroker.

The five towns incorporated into the city of Stoke-on-Trent—Turnstall, Burslem, Hanley, Stoke, and Longton—are Turnhill, Bursley, Hanbridge, Knype, and Longshaw in Bennett's novels of the Five Towns. Many of the landmarks within the towns have been identified with places in his works; however, urban development is slowly diminishing the list of existing structures. The **Arnold Bennett Museum** has a catalog of those places still standing.

Bennett spent much time at and was greatly influenced by the shop at the corner of St. John's Square and William Clowes Street, in Burslem (Bursley in the novels), which was owned by his maternal grandparents, the Longsons; it appears in *The Old Wives' Tale* as John Baine's Shop. Here he was under an even stronger Wesleyan influence than at home. Also, many references to houses and residents in Waterloo Road, Cobridge, are to be found in the novels.

(Bennett House open Mon., Wed., Thurs., Sat. 2–5. Free.)

STRATFORD-UPON-AVON   (Warwickshire)

Shakespeare's Birthplace, Stratford-upon-Avon, is probably visited by more tourists than any other place outside London. Most of the buildings associated with the great dramatist have been restored, and, except for the modern brick theater, the atmosphere of the Elizabethan market town that Shakespeare knew some three-and-a-half centuries ago still prevails.

The reputed birthplace is a small room on the first floor of a half-timbered sixteenth-century building on Henley Street. In Shakespeare's time the property consisted of two separate buildings—one the Shakespeare family home and the other a shop or adjoining warehouse, which the poet's father, John Shakespeare, used in his business as a glover and wool dealer. The living quarters—a living room, kitchen, cellar, the birth room, and other upstairs rooms—are furnished in period style, while the remainder of the building is arranged as a museum containing books, manuscripts, and other objects related to Shakespeare's works and the period in which he wrote. The garden has been planted with trees, plants, and flowers mentioned in the poet's plays and poems.

Only the foundations of **New Place,** the house where Shakespeare spent his retirement and died, remain. According to historical records this was one of Stratford's most imposing houses. The entrance to the gardens, in which the foundations are preserved, is through Nash's House, which belonged to Thomas Nash, the first husband of Shakespeare's granddaughter, Elizabeth Hall. Furniture and exhibits in this house depict the background of Shakespeare's England, and the Knott garden adjoining the foundations is a replica of an Elizabethan garden. The Great Garden of New Place, with the foundations, is reached from Chapel Lane. Here is an ancient mulberry tree claimed to have been grown from a cutting of a tree planted by Shakespeare himself.

Hall's Croft, home of Shakespeare's daughter Susanna and her husband, Dr. John Hall, is a half-timbered building beautifully furnished with rare period furniture and exhibits relating to Dr. John Hall and the Stratford Shakespeare Festival. In the back is a spacious walled garden.

Just over a mile from the center of town at Shottery is **Anne Hathaway's Cottage,** the picturesque farmhouse which was the home of Shakespeare's wife, Anne Hathaway, and of the Hathaway family of yeoman farmers. Part of the building dates back to the fifteenth century, and there has been little restoration of its stone, timber frame, wattle, and brick. The orchard and gardens are particularly beautiful, and inside are many of the original Hathaway furnishings and relics.

Mary Arden's House, the Tudor farmhouse where Mary Arden, Shakespeare's mother, lived, is also open. It is located at Wilmcote, a small village three miles from Stratford. Here

Mary Arden was born and lived until she married John Shakespeare and moved to Stratford. Adjoining the house is a charming Old World garden and an interesting museum.

Holy Trinity Church, just off Trinity Street, is a graceful building whose slender spire is reflected in the quietly flowing Avon. The approach to the church is through a long, paved walk bordered by lime trees. Inside are the parish registers containing the entries of Shakespeare's baptism and burial, and his monument and gravestone bearing the famous inscription:

> Good frend for Jesvs sake forebeare
> to digg the dvst encloased heare;
> Blese be ye man yt spares thes stones
> And cvrst be he yt moves my bones.

It is because of these lines that Shakespeare's remains were never removed to Westminster Abbey in London.

Also along the Avon, right in the center of town, is the red-brick **Shakespeare Theatre,** controversial because of its architecture, which opened in 1932. The building has superb facilities for both audience and actors, and puts on performances almost daily during the tourist season. One section of the first Memorial Shakespeare Theatre, the Picture Gallery Wing, destroyed by fire in 1926, remains. This exhibits relics of famous actors and actresses, along with a number of portraits of Shakespeare, paintings illustrating scenes from Shakespeare's plays, and portraits of famous actors and actresses associated with the theater. Each year hundreds of thousands come from all over the world to see Shakespearean productions here, and the Stratford companies visit a number of other countries. The theater also has a London home at the Aldwych Theatre.

(Buildings mentioned above are open Apr.–Oct., weekdays 9–6, Sun. 2–6; Nov.–Mar., shorter hours.)

TINTAGEL   (Cornwall): 2 mi. SW of Bocastle, on B3263

The Department of Ancient Monuments proclaims that no evidence supports the legendary connection of **Tintagel Castle** and King Arthur. The earliest evidence of such a link, they say, is in the works of Geoffrey of Monmouth, who wrote when the first Norman castle was being built. To explain the ruins of the Celtic monastery on the site, he built the Arthurian legend from his vivid imagination.

No one nurtured on the song and legend of King Arthur could have made such a statement. The castle and its surroundings are a classic setting for a medieval romance. True, the castle was built centuries after Arthur lived, and the facts that Arthur was a Celtic hero who fought off the English and that Tintagel was built on the site of a Celtic monastery may be related only by coincidence. But medieval romance and nineteenth-century poetry would be nothing without King Arthur. Even in the twelfth century some of the Cornish hoped that he would come again to save them. Obviously they had not recovered from their last defeat by the English.

Nevertheless, Celtic myth remains, and believers will be spellbound by the "black cliffs and caves and storm and wind" which Tennyson found here and celebrated in *Idylls of the King*. The romantic ruin is set up on a water-ravaged cliff, torn apart where the sea and headland meet. Jagged rocks hang over the cave where the naked baby Arthur was swept in on a wave from the Irish Sea and caught by Merlin the magician. You can also see the spot where the Round Table supposedly met. In any season the sea reigns at Tintagel. Waves lunge against the cliffs, and the strong wind finds its way through the ruins.

The whole island of Tintagel once projected much farther out into the sea. In the twelfth century Geoffrey of Monmouth described it as a mighty fortress surrounded by the sea, with one entrance through the rock so narrow that only a few men could defend it against all of England. Romances a century later mention the receding rock coastline, while fourteenth-century writings describe a bridge between the two sections of the castle. After the sixteenth century the bridge was not kept in repair, and now the island is accessible only by boat. It was during medieval times that the castle became famous for its part in Arthurian romance.

Celtic history puts Arthur at the end of the fifth century, the time when the Saxons were plundering lower Britain. Presumably he was a great leader, perhaps succeeding Roman commanders in defending the country against Germanic tribes. In fact, there really seem to have been two Arthurs, one defending England against invaders from the sea and another warding off the more barbaric Celts from the northern hills and Wales. Later, as the Celts settled back into the more northern parts of the island, the southerners, especially the Cornish, still glorified Arthur as their savior from war. During the Dark Ages Arthur became a more mystical hero with the Celts, and his legend became embellished with Christian and pagan ritual. Thus there emerged a popular Arthurian legend by the beginning of the twelfth century. Geoffrey of Monmouth's *History of the Britains* made Arthur universally popular.

Tintagel in that work was the fortress of the Duke of Cornwall, Gorlois, who locked up his wife, Ygraine, there while the British king Uther was invading the country. While the duke was shut up in a neighboring castle (perhaps Boscastle), Uther, with Merlin the magician's help, disguised himself as the duke and entered Tintagel to seduce Ygraine. The duke soon died, and then Arthur was born. The fact that the same story appears in the French romance of Merlin and in the Grail romance "Perceval li Gallois" implies that Geoffrey adapted the already established legend to the Tintagel he knew.

Later on, in the nineteenth century, Arthur reigned supreme. Tennyson's poems about the "early paradise Tintagel" made the legend popular again. After that came many modern versions of Arthur's story, and Tintagel appeared in almost every illustration of works about King Arthur. About the same time repair of the castle began, and the whole area was placed under government control.

(Tintagel Castle is open May–Sept., weekdays 9:30–7, Sun. 2–5:30; closes an hour earlier rest of year. Nominal charge.)

TITCHFIELD   (Hampshire): 10 mi. E of Southampton

Shakespeare, according to many scholars, came often to nourish his imagination at the now derelict **Titchfield Abbey,** and is thought to have written here an early comedy, *Love's Labour's Lost*, to amuse a nearby country household at Christmastime.

TUNBRIDGE WELLS   (Kent): 30 mi. SW of London on A21

From 1606, when wells were discovered in a hilly district of Kent, until the Regency period, when it was superseded by Brighton, Tunbridge Wells was the chief resort of London intellectuals. Its fashionable drawing rooms were described by Thackeray in *The Virginians* and *Henry Esmond*, and it is easy to visualize scenes from the novels when you stroll around the town. In fact, Tunbridge Wells is often thought of as Thackeray's town in the same sense that Broadstairs belongs to Dickens. Thackeray's own square Georgian house, marked by a plaque, can be seen on the other side of the common from Ephraim's. During the town's peak, England's most famous master of ceremonies, the dandy Beau Nash, left Bath to come here. Other frequent visitors to Tunbridge Wells were Colley Cibber, Samuel Johnson, David Garrick, and Joshua Reynolds. The Tennysons lived here for a time too.

UPPARK   (West Sussex): 5 mi. SE of Petersfield on B2146

Much of H. G. Wells's youth was spent at Uppark, the seventeenth-century mansion in Sussex where his mother was a housekeeper. The house, strikingly symmetrical in shape and constructed of mellow red brick, stands on the summit of the South Downs above the village of South Harting, very close to the Sussex-Hampshire border. The hill that it crowns is nearly 600 feet above sea level and rises steeply about 300 feet from the valleys below. In the mid-eighteenth century the house was bought by a wealthy baronet who traveled extensively and assembled a fine collection of furniture, pictures, and other objets d'art, shipped them to England, and conveyed them here by oxcart. Thus Uppark has one of the finest saloons and several of the most elaborate staterooms of any country house in England.

The novelist's mother came here sometime after 1870 and stayed as housekeeper for about thirteen years. In his novel *Tono Bungay,* published in 1909, the house Blazeover is based on his recollections of Uppark. Wells spoke of their stay there as a time of good fortune, a time when he was free to experiment with all sorts of things. On one occasion during a fortnight's snowstorm he produced a newspaper on kitchen paper and performed a shadow play for the maids and others in a miniature theater he had made in the housekeeper's room. As he looked back to his days there, he recalled that the place had a great effect on him, that there was a kind of vitality within the servants' quarters which contrasted with the routines of the aristocracy around them. He felt that one of the finest attributes of the house, aside from the great collections and the community within, which he knew intimately, was the incomparable view over miles of wooded downland, descending gradually to the coastal plain and sea.

WARNHAM   (Sussex): 4 mi. NW of Horsham, just west of A24

Romantic poet Percy Bysshe Shelley was born at **Field Place,** a manor near Warnham, in 1792. The long, low white house, surrounded by parkland, is now privately occupied and not open to visitors, but still looks essentially as it did during his childhood. When Shelley came home to Field Place from Eton College, he was refused admission by his father, a conventional country squire who had little understanding of his rebellious son. Shelley stayed out among the trees all night, reading Milton's poetry, until a kindly servant awoke the next morning and let him in for breakfast.

WHITBY   (North Yorkshire): on A171, 40 mi. E of Darlington

Coastal Whitby is often linked with the world-famous sailor and explorer Captain Cook. The house in which he lived during his three-year apprenticeship to a master seaman is open as a museum. Writer Elizabeth Gaskell spent time in Whitby too and vividly described life here in *Sylvia's Lovers*. Her backdrop included the strange little jetties, backyards convenient for smuggling, and a number of ancient hostelries—including the White Horse Inn, where seamen once gathered to discuss Cook's latest adventures. Several of the incidents she relates, especially those about press-gang activities, are authentic and were passed on to her by a local banking family.

WINCHESTER

A number of writers have associations in and around this town. Those who claim that Anthony Trollope's *The Warden* is based on Winchester rather than Salisbury say that **St. Cross Hospital** is Hiram's Hospital, where the Warden goes to ask for the medieval dole of bread and ale. Winchester is Wintonchester in Thomas Hardy's *Tess of the D'Urbervilles,* and the placid south-country scenery around Winchester inspired John Keats to write his beautiful "Ode to Autumn." Both Jane Austen and Izaak Walton, author of *The Compleat Angler,* are buried in **Winchester Cathedral.** In Prior Silkestede's Chapel there is a stained-glass window dedicated to Walton. Given by fishermen of many lands, the window depicts biblical scenes of God rewarding men with fish, and includes portraits of Walton in each lower corner. There is also a stained-glass window and plaque near Jane Austen's burial place. The house where she died on **College Street,** after coming from Chawton to be treated by a doctor, is also marked by a memorial tablet.

WINDSOR   (Berkshire): 20 mi. W of London on M4

Shakespeare set his *Merry Wives of Windsor* at **Frogmore,** a manor in the forest that adjoins Windsor Great Park. The estate can be viewed over the fence by walking through the gate of the park and several hundred yards along the tree-lined path.

YORK   (Yorkshire): 20 mi. NW of Leeds

York has changed little since the first mystery plays were put on in medieval times. The most famous of these pieces of early English drama is *The Corpus Christi Play,* which originally began on the streets of this city and is now reenacted each summer as part of the city's Festival of the Arts.

Evidence from York and elsewhere shows that the plays were first written by clerics and acted out as single performances within the church, often to celebrate certain Christian celebrations, and were later combined into longer productions as they became more secular. From the early fourteenth century to the late sixteenth century, a procession of wagons, or pageants, threaded its way through the streets on Corpus Christi Day. Each pageant bore the actors and the set of a short play, and all the plays together formed the narrative of Christian history from the Creation to the Last Judgment, the climax of which was the Passion and Resurrection. The pageants stopped at different stations in the streets and performed for the residents of York and out-of-town visitors, who often included royalty.

By the time of the organized Corpus Christi Day celebration the presentation of the series of mystery plays was the responsibility of the city's mayor, who delegated individual plays to certain trade guilds, and members were actually liable to fines for defective sets or bad acting. Often there would be a thematic connection between a trade guild and its play. The shipwrights performed *Noah and the Ark,* while the goldsmiths put on *The Three Kings* and the butchers *The Crucifixion of Christ.* York was a prosperous medieval city, and records indicate elaborate financial arrangements for the staging of these plays.

London

AROUND THE OLD CITY OF LONDON

On Gracechurch Street, in front of the present-day Monument Underground Station, was the Boar's Head Tavern where Prince Hal caroused in Shakespeare's *Henry IV*. From across London Bridge you can get a good view of the Monument, built to commemorate the thousands of lives lost in the Great Fire of 1666, which swallowed up so much of London along the north side of the Thames. Samuel Pepys gave a very vivid account of the fire in his *Diary*.

Just opposite the corner of Gracechurch and Fenchurch streets is **Lombard Street.** A bit down on this street, going west, is **Plough Court,** where Alexander Pope was born. At 71 Lombard Street is Lloyd's Bank, where poet T. S. Eliot worked as a clerk for many years. Right near the bank was the fashionable club Pontack's, often frequented by John Evelyn, Christopher Wren, and Jonathan Swift. Maria Beadnell, Dickens' first serious love, lived at No. 2 in a residence over her father's bank. Maria was forbidden to see Dickens, since at the time of their courtship he was a very poor law clerk, but their prolific correspondence of several years is preserved, and can be seen at the Dickens House and Museum on Doughty Street. Evidently Maria kept giving him false hopes over a long period of time, knowing that her father would never allow her to become engaged to such an unsuitable gentleman.

143

Just around the corner at 35 **Cornhill** is a plaque and portrait of Thomas Gray, who was born here in 1716. "The Curfew tolls the knell of parting day," the beginning line of his "Elegy in a Country Churchyard," is inscribed on the tablet. Nearby in the Church of St. Michael is Gray's silver-headed cane. Across the street at No. 32 is the Cornhill Insurance Company, whose intricately carved doors have a panel showing a meeting of the Brontë sisters, Charlotte and Anne, with William Makepeace Thackeray. The encounter took place in 1847, the year that *Wuthering Heights* and *Jane Eyre* were published. To the north, just up a little on King Street, is the entrance to **Lawrence Lane.** Over an archway there is a carved head of Sam Weller of Dickens' *Pickwick Papers.* Dickens often credited him with an extensive and peculiar knowledge of London.

Here on the **Poultry,** as the section of the street between Cornhill and Cheapside is named, were some of the most famous taverns frequented by literary figures of the pre-Restoration period. A number of noted eighteenth-century booksellers were located here also, and among their successful works was Boswell's biography of Johnson. Just at the point where the Poultry meets Queen Victoria Street is the Midland Bank, with a plaque indicating that it is the site of Thomas Hood's birthplace. Its inscription reads, "I remember, I remember, the house where I was born."

At the Bank of England, opposite the Mansion House, two famous writers of children's literature were once clerks: Kenneth Grahame, author of *The Wind in the Willows,* and A. A. Milne, who wrote *Toad of Toad Hall,* a dramatization of Grahame's book, and *Winnie-the-Pooh.* The bank is mentioned in the introduction to *The Wind in the Willows:* "Reading these lovely visions of childhood, you might have wondered that he could be so mixed up in anything so unlovely as a bank; and it may be presumed at the bank an equal surprise was felt that such a responsible official could be mixed up with such beauty." A block behind the Bank of England, to the east at Moorgate, is a memorial to rural poet Robert Bloomfield on the wall of Kent House.

In this area is **Guildhall,** seat of government for the City of London. Part of the fifteenth-century building still survives,

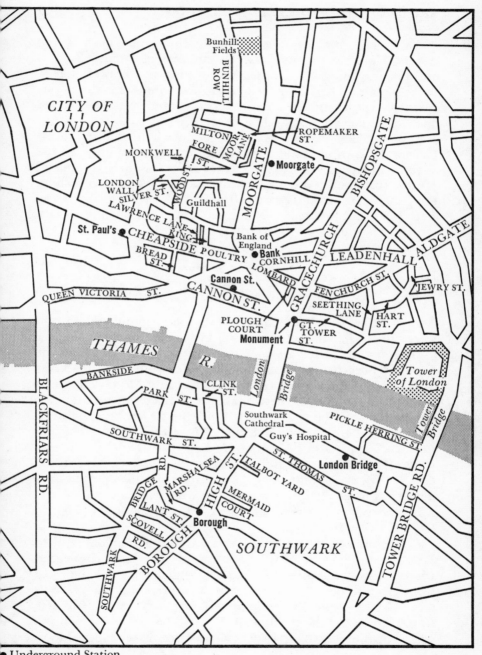

● Underground Station

and the crypt and magnificent Tudor library are open to the public. Here are manuscripts of a number of famous English authors, including the first, second, and fourth folios of Shakespeare's plays. The library's stained-glass windows contain pictures of Milton and Wynkyn de Worde, and busts of Chaucer and Tennyson are on the library steps.

Coming back through King Street to where Poultry meets Cheapside, **Bird in Hand Court** opens on the south side. At the back of this court, at No. 76, Keats wrote his first volume of poems. Just at the corner of Cheapside and Wood streets stood the famous Mermaid Tavern, often frequented by Shakespeare, Ben Jonson, Christopher Marlowe, and John Donne. Keats, writing his sonnet on Chapman's Homer, asked:

> Souls of poets have dead and gone,
> What Elysium have ye known,
> Happy field or mossy cavern
> Choicer than the Mermaid Tavern?

Across the way in **Bread Street** both John Donne and Milton were born. The alleged birthplaces are marked by plaques.

By going north for a few blocks on Wood Street, where the Cavalier poet Robert Herrick was born, you come to **Silver Street** on the west; at the corner of Silver and Monkwell streets was Mountjoy House, where Shakespeare lived during the years he wrote many of his best plays. While he stayed here, between 1598 and 1604, he wrote *Henry V, The Merry Wives of Windsor, Much Ado About Nothing, As You Like It, All's Well that Ends Well, Julius Caesar, Hamlet, Measure for Measure, Othello, Macbeth,* and *King Lear*. Proof of Shakespeare's residence was unearthed by an American scholar, William Wallace, while he was going through dusty documents at the English Record Office in 1909.

Continuing north on Wood Street through London Wall to **Fore Street,** you come to the Church of St. Giles Cripplegate, where Milton is buried. His statue, which once stood in the front, is now at the Cripplegate Institute, but his grave is marked by a stone on the floor near the altar, and there is a simple bust near the south wall. Daniel Defoe was born in the parish of the church in 1659. Where Fore Street meets Moorgate stands the Moorgate Public House, with a plaque stating that John Keats was born in the Swan and Hoop, which formerly stood there.

Branching north off Fore Street is Moor Lane, which takes you to **Milton Street**. This, the Grub Street of Pope's obloquy, was the home of impoverished writers during the eighteenth century. Dr. Johnson spoke of it as the street inhabited by writers "of small histories, dictionaries, and temporary poems."

Just across from Milton Street is **Ropemaker Street,** formerly Ropemaker Alley, where Daniel Defoe died while hiding from some unknown danger. The west end of Ropemaker Street leads into Moor Lane, which in turns leads into **Bunhill Row.** It was at No. 125 on this street that Milton died. Here, before the outbreak of the Great Plague, he wrote *Paradise Lost* and lived with his young second wife, who acted as companion and amanuensis for the blind poet. After the publication of that great work, visitors from all over came to wander around **Bunhill Fields,** always hoping to encounter the frail blind man who often sat on his front steps or meandered around the streets. In the adjacent Nonconformist cemetery of Bunhill Fields, John Bunyan, Daniel Defoe, Isaac Watts, and William Blake lie. "Nonconformist" generally meant those who did not conform to the Church of England or constitutional authority. About one hundred feet or so in on the left is the tomb of John Bunyan, and to the right of that is a dark obelisk, marking the grave of Daniel Defoe. Mystical poet William Blake's small, blackened slab is also nearby. His body was one not accepted at Westminster Abbey.

BRITISH MUSEUM AREA

There is no end to literary associations at the **British Museum.** You could spend days in the first floor Manuscript Salon and in King's Library, lifting the dark cloths off the display cases and peering in to read the well-preserved papers. There are ancient manuscripts of Beowulf and Chaucer, *Sir Gawain and the Green Knight, Piers Plowman,* one of the earliest *Book of*

Kings Cross ●
St. Pancras

EUSTON ROAD

Euston ●

Euston Sq. ●

TAVISTOCK PL.

Coram Fields

GRAY'S INN RD.

DOUGHTY ST.

Tavistock
Sq.

CORAM ST.

WOBURN PL.

BEDFORD W.

Gordon
Sq.

● Russell Sq.

Russell
Sq.

SOUTHAMPTON

BLOOMSBURY

THEOBALD'S RD.

*Gray's
Inn
Gardens*

British
Museum

TOTTENHAM COURT

Goodge St. ●

HIGH HOLBORN

Holborn ●

NEW OXFORD ST.

KINGSWAY

Tottenham Court Rd. ●

● Underground Station

Hours, first folios of Shakespeare; scores of more recent holo-
graph manuscripts, among them Eliot's *The Mill on the Floss,*
Hardy's *Tess of the D'Urbervilles,* Joyce's *Finnegans Wake,*
Pepys's *Diary,* and scores more noted holograph letters by
famous authors. You can stand here to read John Donne's letter
from prison, Charles Lamb's description of his dinner with
Wordsworth, or Charles Darwin's defense of his *The Origin
of Species.* Then, of course, near the entrance is the Rosetta
Stone, key to translating Egyptian hieroglyphics. In the Duveen
Gallery are the Elgin Marbles, which inspired John Keats to
write his famous "Ode to a Grecian Urn."

Many famous writers have lived in the tall gray town houses
on **Russell Square,** just behind the museum. Ralph Waldo
Emerson stayed at No. 63 when he came to London in 1833.
Writer Mary Russell Mitford lived at No. 56 and often had
William Wordsworth and Walter Savage Landor as her guests.
T. S. Eliot used No. 24 as his London address for many years
when he was an editor for the publishing firm of Faber and
Faber, which had its offices there. Thackeray even set part of
Vanity Fair on this square. The Osbornes lived at No. 96 and
the Sedleys at No. 62.

Much has been written on the lives of the famous Bloomsbury group, which was centered around **Gordon Square** at the
turn of the century. Recent biographies of Lytton Strachey and
Virginia Woolf describe in detail the everyday lives of the
brilliant and artistic men and women who lived here. Virginia
Stephen Woolf and Vanessa Stephen Bell, daughters of Sir
Leslie Stephen, were longtime members of the group, as were
editor and historian Leonard Woolf, husband of Virginia, and
Clive Bell, art and literary critic, husband of Vanessa.

No. 46 Gordon Square was where the Bloomsbury circle first
became acquainted. When their father, Leslie Stephen, died,
Virginia, Vanessa, and their two brothers, Thoby and Adrian,
leased the house and moved here from their parents' rather in-
hibiting home in Kensington. Here the intellectual associations
began, with Thoby Stephen bringing home his Cambridge
friends. Soon Leonard Woolf, Clive Bell, Lytton Strachey, Maynard Keynes, and others began meeting to talk into the morning
hours. Even after Vanessa and Virginia married and moved to

other nearby houses, No. 46 remained the center of activity for the group. John Maynard Keynes and his wife, the dancer Lydia Lopokova, lived there after them. Then for a while artist Duncan Grant lived with the Bells at No. 37 and at No. 50, which was also at times the residence of Adrian Stephen and his wife.

A block north through Bedford West is **Tavistock Square,** where Charles Dickens lived for ten years at Tavistock House, which stood on the square's northeast corner, and wrote *Hard Times, Little Dorrit,* and *A Tale of Two Cities.* In his back garden he erected a small theater and staged productions, often playing a leading part himself. Years later Virginia and Leonard Woolf settled at No. 52 and set up the Hogarth Press in their basement. Here they printed the first editions of T. S. Eliot's *Waste Land.* Both the Dickens and Woolf houses were bombed out during the war, and the Tavistock Hotel has been built on the site of the Woolf residence. Across Woburn Place on **Coram Street,** one block south of Tavistock Place, Thackeray lived in poverty at No. 13. Richard Le Gallienne, poet and critic of the aesthetic movement, lived at No. 49.

CHELSEA

Sloane Square Station is a good place to begin a walking tour of Chelsea's literary spots. Just to the right on the square is the **Royal Court Theatre,** famous for having produced many plays of George Bernard Shaw, Somerset Maugham, and John Galsworthy earlier in the century.

Lower Sloane Street across the square leads down to Royal Hospital Road, where the **Royal Hospital** for disabled veterans is located. Though Nell Gwyn supposedly encouraged her lover Charles II to found the hospital, diarist John Evelyn was more important in its establishment. Dr. John Arbuthnot, satirical writer and friend of Swift and Pope, and the one to whom Pope's famous poem "Epistle to Dr. Arbuthnot" is addressed, was chief physician here. Thomas Hardy often came here to see the military museum and talk to the old soldiers in order to get

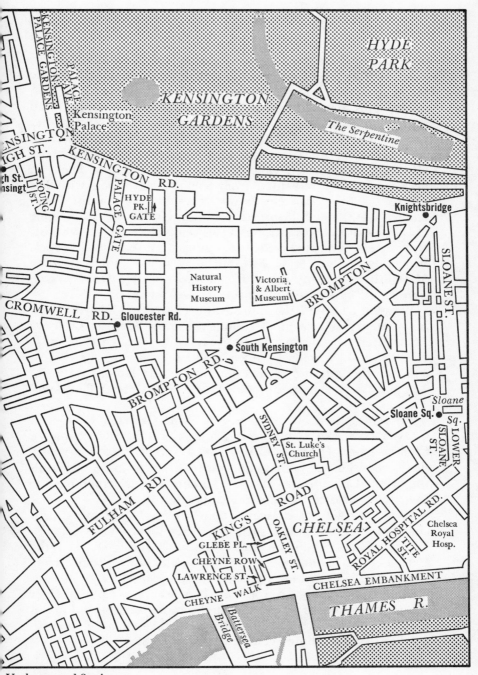

Underground Station

material for *The Dynasts,* his drama of the Napoleonic Wars.

At 34 **Tite Street,** the third street down from Lower Sloane Street on the right, Oscar Wilde lived while he wrote his greatest works. This area between the River Thames and King's Road is plentiful with names of famous writers. Several blocks farther down Royal Hospital Road becomes **Cheyne Walk,** separated from the river for two more long blocks by groups of trees. George Eliot's house, No. 4, is marked with a plaque. She died here weeks after returning from a long honeymoon with her husband John Cross. No. 6 was the home of novelist C. P. Snow's wife, Pamela Hansford Johnson. No. 20, long the home of Dante Gabriel Rossetti, was a gathering place for many artists and writers associated with the aesthetic movement—Whistler, Browning, Wilde, A. C. Swinburne, William Morris, George Meredith, and many more. Don Satero's Coffee House, often frequented by eighteenth-century writers, stood at No. 18.

Between Cheyne Row and Lawrence Street on Cheyne Walk is a pretentious apartment complex, **Carlyle Mansions.** Henry James lived here during the last years of his life. Later both T. S. Eliot and Arnold Toynbee made their homes here. Just opposite the entrance to Cheyne Row is the famous statue of Thomas Carlyle, nestled in the shrubbery of the traffic island.

An atmosphere of greatness lingers at **Carlyle's House,** 24 Cheyne Row, an old Queen Anne house in the center of Chelsea where Thomas Carlyle lived and worked for nearly fifty years. This is perhaps the only "literary house" with all the original furnishings intact. The entire house embodies the Victorian world of the Carlyles as they left it.

In the cozy front drawing room are the same overstuffed chairs and sofas on which such illustrious Victorians as Chopin, Dickens, Hunt, Tennyson, and Emerson sat and talked with the Carlyles for many hours. Leigh Hunt's well-known poem "Jenny Kissed Me" is based on a greeting he once received from Mrs. Carlyle as she sprang up from her chair here to greet him. Over the chimneypiece is a painting of the room as it looked about that time. The Carlyles had just installed a new fireplace with a fashionable Brahmin gate and Dutch tiles.

The most noteworthy Carlyle material can be seen in his third-floor attic study. The author built this "soundproof" room at the top of the house in 1853 so that he could work undisturbed by the noises from the street and neighboring houses and gardens. You can see the passage dividing the inner and outer walls and the skylight with sliding sash windows. Unfortunately, the clever design failed, but Carlyle used the so-called silent room as his study for twelve years until 1865, when he finished *Frederick the Great*. On exhibit here are many sections from his manuscripts, a few personal relics, and the worktable on which he wrote most of his books.

The second-floor guest room is of special interest to Americans because Emerson, who was so influenced by Carlyle, stayed here while visiting. All the rooms, in fact, deserve careful contemplation, not so much because they reveal the bourgeois lifestyle of a renowned author, but for their aura of authenticity. Nothing seems restored or arranged by a curator. Mrs. Carlyle's doilies are still on the chairs and her bric-a-brac here and there on the shelves. The oak paneling, which the Carlyles had papered and lacquered to resemble mahogany, remains as they left it. Carlyle's friends were often amazed that a man of such eminence could remain content in these surroundings throughout his life. Perhaps contrasting this house to his family's humble cottage in Ecclefechan makes such contentment understandable.

At 96 **Cheyne Walk** Whistler painted the famous portraits of his mother and Carlyle. From the house you can walk up Cheyne Row to Glebe Place, which leads to King's Road through Oakley Street. This block of **King's Road** has a number of literary houses. Somerset Maugham made his home at No. 213, and at No. 215 lived Ellen Terry, famous actress and good friend of George Bernard Shaw. Samuel Richardson lived for many years and died at No. 247.

On **Sydney Street,** which runs directly north across from Town Hall, is St. Luke's Church, built in the 1820's, an example of the Romantic movement's passion for Gothic and medieval revival, brought on largely by the popular novels and poems of Sir Walter Scott. Novelist Charles Kingsley was curate here for a time, and Charles Dickens married Catherine Hogarth here in 1836. No. 36 was once the home of Bertrand Russell.

FLEET STREET and DR. JOHNSON

Fleet Street has long been called "the Street of Scribblers" for its associations with printing and journalism. A good place to begin a walk of this area is the point where Fleet Street and Middle Temple Lane meet. At No. 1 is Child's Bank, which has been there since its founding in 1674 and has had such well-known clients as Defoe and Dryden. The original building was the Tellson's Bank of *A Tale of Two Cities,* and was, according to Dickens, "very small, very dark, very ugly, very incommodious," and "the triumphant perfection of inconvenience." Just across the street stood the famous Cock Tavern, where Samuel Pepys came to meet and charm women, and which headwaiter Alfred Tennyson later celebrated in his poetry. Dickens often frequented its successor, the Cock Tavern at No. 17. In his chosen corner, in what is now called the Dickens Room, the plate he used is still preserved. The Devil Tavern, a well-known haunt for eighteenth-century poets, was also on this block. Here Ben Jonson helped form the Apollo Club, one of England's first literary groups. And just a few doors down on the east side of Fleet Street, at No. 37, was the Mitre Tavern, now Hoare's Bank, where Samuel Johnson and Oliver Goldsmith used to meet.

Falcon Court, the next street to the right after Inner Temple Lane, is the site of Wynkyn de Worde's sixteenth-century printing shop, The Falcon. *Gorboduc,* England's first tragedy, was printed here. A bit farther down, at No. 39 was The Mitre bookstore, where Milton's *Paradise Regained* and *Samson Agonistes* were first sold in 1671. A few years later the Blue Anchor, another store close by, began selling Milton's poems.

Just off Fleet Street in Wine Office Court is the Cheshire Cheese, the renowned restaurant where Dr. Johnson, Boswell, Goldsmith, and the rest of the Johnson circle met regularly.

Johnson's portrait dominates the head table. A room on the second floor was frequented by the Rhymers Club of the 1890's —Arthur Symons, Ernest Dowson, W. B. Yeats, and others. No. 6 Wine Office Court was the home of Oliver Goldsmith while he was writing *The Vicar of Wakefield*. It is said that Goldsmith discussed the progress of the novel many times as they sat there at the Cheshire Cheese, and that on its completion Johnson whisked it off to a bookseller and sold it for sixty guineas, just in time to keep Goldsmith from being arrested for not paying his rent.

Johnson's House stands farther on through the winding court-yard in Gough Square. Here the great lexicographer lived from 1748 to 1758, compiling his famous dictionary in the garret. His biographer, Boswell, who did not know him while he lived here, ascertained that the room was "fitted up like a counting house," with clerks writing assiduously as they leaned over the long table strewn with papers. Although Johnson employed six clerks (five of whom were Scotsmen), they apparently did not help with the research. He often toiled here for over twenty-four hours at a time without relief during the ten-year period that the project went on. During the last few years he lost two of the clerks to illness and had to take over their work also. There were four editions of the dictionary in his lifetime. With revisions it remained the standard English dictionary for about a hundred years, before the *Oxford Dictionary* took its place.

The garret is now bare and clean, with beams protruding from carefully whitewashed walls. Visitors must imagine the busy scene here over two hundred years ago. Joshua Reynolds once described a visit to this room, which Johnson also con-sidered his library. Besides Johnson's books, covered with a thick layer of dust, was a crazy old card table, and an even older elbow chair with only three legs.

There are no original furnishings in the house. After Dr. Johnson left, it was occupied by tenants until its restoration in 1911. Throughout, however, are many valuable oil paintings which reveal much of Johnson's world. In the dining room and parlor hang portraits of those close to the author, among them actor David Garrick, whom he considered a master of the stage;

his companion and biographer, James Boswell; and dramatist Richard Brinsley Sheridan. Also here is the famous oil of Dr. Johnson reading Goldsmith's *The Vicar of Wakefield*. Scattered among the other paintings which line the walls of the room from the first to the third floor are innumerable likenesses of Johnson and copies of the famous Joshua Reynolds portrait.

On the landing is Goodman's sketch of Lichfield, Dr. Johnson's birthplace. The handboard you are given upon entering has a comprehensive account of his life in that town before he came to London at age twenty-eight. In the library, possibly once Dr. Johnson's bedroom, is Catherine Read's painting of Elizabeth Carter, the bluestocking whom Johnson so admired for her intellectual accomplishments.

Until Johnson came to Gough Square he had led a wretched existence. His poem "London," an imitation of Juvenal's satire on Rome, had made his talent evident to the booksellers who commissioned him to do the dictionary. It was then that he came to Gough Square to lead a life of hard work with a bit of personal tragedy. While he was working on his colossal task his devoted wife, Tetty, died, leaving him lonely and heartsick. Several times he was carried off to debtors' prison until he was rescued by Samuel Richardson, the novelist and printer.

It was from this house that he wrote to Lord Chesterfield, who had snubbed him years before and, now that Johnson was famous, was anxious to be his patron. Johnson replied, "The notice which you have been pleased to take of my labors, had it been early, had been kind; but it has been delayed till I am indifferent, and cannot enjoy it; till I am solitary, and cannot impart it; till I am known, and do not want it."

(Johnson's House is open all year daily except Sun. and bank holidays, May–Sept. 10:30–5; Apr.–Oct. 10:30–4:30; nominal charge.)

Back through Wine Office Court and across Fleet Street is **St. Bride's Church,** novelist Samuel Richardson's burial place. Rebuilt by Wren after the Great Fire, and then destroyed by the Blitz in World War II, the church has been restored very closely to Wren's original drawings. During excavations for rebuilding the church the skeleton buried before the altar of

St. Catherine was identified almost positively as that of Wynkyn de Worde.

St. Bride's has long been a journalist's church. In fact, the Press Association and Reuters were responsible for its renovation after World War II. The basement has, in addition to the crypts, a photographic exhibit of the church's restoration and an illustrated narrative of the growth of the publishing industry since the Middle Ages. Richardson's coffin is in a crypt discovered during the postwar restoration, along with those of his two wives and a few relatives. Behind the pipes at one end are the remains of a sixth-century church, the apse of its ninth-century successor, and remains of a twelfth-century Norman church. Shadows of John Milton still lurk in the churchyard. On this site one of his houses stood; here he brought his first bride and educated his two fatherless nephews before moving to Aldersgate Street.

GRAY'S INN and CHANCERY

Dickens House and Museum on Doughty Street is one of the most comprehensive, and certainly one of the most popular, literary museums in England. The Dickens Fellowship, devoted entirely to the study of Dickens and his works, has it as its headquarters here—appropriately so, since it is also very important as an author's house. Dickens came here early in his career and wrote the three major novels which put him well on the road to success. In addition to the study, where he created such immortal characters as Fagin, Bill Sikes, and the Artful Dodger, there are a number of rooms filled with personal relics, sections from original manuscripts, first editions, and important letters.

The first-floor dining room was the scene of many parties for the literary and artistic celebrities of Dickens' time. Here his first great literary friend, W. Harrison Ainsworth, introduced him to his first publisher, John Macone, and to his first illustrator, the famous George Cruikshank. Standing ominously near the front window amid other period furniture is the grandfather

clock that belonged to Moses Pickwick, the original of Mr.
Pickwick, proprietor of the White Hart Inn in Bath.

In the upstairs study, where he wrote *Pickwick Papers, Oliver
Twist,* and most of *Nicholas Nickleby,* is the desk he used at his
last and most elaborate residence, the mansion Cobham Hall
at Gad's Hill Place. Also there is the Dr. Henry collection,
comprising most of the books first published in monthly-paper
parts and a page of the manuscript for *Oliver Twist;* but perhaps most interesting are the sections of the *Nicholas Nickleby*
manuscript and his correspondence with illustrator Cruikshank
and printer Hicks as he was conceiving the novel. He told them
he was planning an intensive journey to study the Yorkshire
schools in preparation for writing an exposé of educational prac-
tices there.

The adjoining room houses the invaluable Dickens Reference
Library, largely consisting of the F. F. Kitton and B. W. Matz
collections, in addition to many letters and autographs. Of special interest here is a letter to his friend Harrison Ainsworth
which further explains his motives for writing *Nicholas
Nickleby.* Of special note too is the small room in which his
young sister-in-law Mary Hogarth died. Possibly her death inspired the scene of Rose Mayfield's near-fatal fever in *Oliver
Twist* and certain aspects of Little Nell in *The Old Curiosity
Shop.* Mary was an integral part of the Dickens family circle
and her death was a great setback to Dickens. In fact, after her
passing he was unable to write for a number of months. In the
same room is the desk on which he worked as a lawyer's clerk
at Gray's Inn, where he picked up a lot of the background for
Bleak House. Dickens' most prized possession, on a table between the second and third floors, is the china monkey he stood
on his desk wherever he happened to be. Without it he could
not settle down to work.

The Suzannet Rooms house a valuable collection of letters
and manuscripts collected by the Count Alain De Suzannet, a
great patron of Dickens House. Included is the entire manuscript of *Nicholas Nickleby,* a page from the manuscript of
Pickwick Papers, and a complete set of the monthly parts of that
work. Much of the collection consists of material relating to
Maria Beadnell, a pretty banker's daughter with whom young

and poverty-stricken Dickens fell passionately in love; but her prudent parents effectively discouraged the match. There are verses and letters exchanged by the two in addition to personal memorabilia connected with their relationship.

Among the fascinating letters on display are a comic rhymed note to Hicks the printer, with some copy for *Pickwick Papers,* and a letter to friend William Jerdan describing the eccentricities of Hans Christian Andersen, who visited the Dickens family in 1857. Also on view is a rich collection of drawings done for his novels by such artists as H. K. Browne (Phiz) and Marcus Stone. Dickens' passion for amateur theatricals may be seen in the numerous playbills. Not only was he a gifted actor, but he also proved a most efficient producer and stage manager for charity performances both in London and in the provinces. His personal reading copies here show how he worked over the texts of his novels to adapt parts of them for the stage.

The basement of the house further illustrates Dickens' world. Here is a reproduction of the Dingley Dell kitchen where Pickwickians made merry at Manor Farm. On the wall in another room are the actual attic windows Dickens gazed through as a boy in Camden Town and the pantry window from his boyhood home in Chertsey, through which Oliver Twist was supposed to have been put by Bill Sikes during the burglary scene. Also on view are a model of the Maypole Inn at Chigwell, as described by Dickens in *Barnaby Rudge,* and the goldbeater's stone from the Soho factory of *A Tale of Two Cities.* Farther on, in the stillroom, where preserves and food supplies were kept, is the stuffed raven immortalized in *Barnaby Rudge.*

(Dickens House is open all year daily, except Sun., bank holidays, and Christmas week, 10–5; nominal charge.)

From Dickens House you can go north to the Coram's Fields area (see "British Museum Area") or take the following walk south:

Just down Gray's Inn Road from Dickens House is **Gray's Inn Gardens,** whose tranquillity was praised in the works of Samuel Pepys and Charles Lamb. Sir Walter Raleigh and Francis Bacon also spent much time here. At the corner of

Gray's Inn Road and High Holborn is the picturesque **Staple Inn,** formerly an Inn of Chancery, where Samuel Johnson lived before moving to his house on Gough Square. From the courtyard of these half-timbered sixteenth-century buildings you can peer up to the apartments above. Dr. Johnson wrote *Rasselas,* completed in two weeks to pay his mother's burial expenses, while living here at No. 2. Wordsworth lived here for a while too, and the inn also appears in Dickens' *Bleak House* and *Edwin Drood.*

Chancery Lane, with all of its Dickens associations, is just a block west of Staple Inn. Down the lane on the east is Cursitor Street, which leads to **Took's Court.** In the nineteenth century there was a sponging house, a kind of halfway house for debtors, on this site. Rawdon Crawley of Thackeray's *Vanity Fair* and Mr. Snogsby of Dickens' *Bleak House* were contained here, as was dramatist Richard Brinsley Sheridan, who spent the last year of his life here.

Another block down toward Fleet Street is the **Public Record Office,** a depository for legal records. Here are letters of Sir Walter Scott, James Boswell, Ben Jonson, John Milton, Francis Bacon, and Edmund Spenser, a manuscript of Shelley's, and signatures on documents by such notables as Shakespeare and Bunyan.

Back up Chancery Lane is a gate which leads over through New Square to **Lincoln's Inn Fields.** This broad square, laid out by Inigo Jones in 1618, is supposed to be the same size as the base of a Great Pyramid. Milton once lived in a house here, as did Dante Gabriel Rossetti, Alfred Tennyson, Charles Dickens, and his Mr. Tulkinghorn of *Bleak House.* Here, in the oldest library in London—founded by the Benchers' of Lincoln's Inn—Oliver Goldsmith, Benjamin Disraeli, Oliver Cromwell, Sir Thomas More, and John Donne, among others, have studied. According to Samuel Pepys's diary, Lincoln's Inn Fields was also the place to come and watch the fashions. After church he and his wife would go "to observe the fashions of the ladies because of my wife making some clothes." The elegant gardens still remain even though the ladies of fashion have long since disappeared. Old Square dates back to 1524. The fine Tudor gatehouse of the inn was built a few years earlier, when poet and dramatist Ben Jonson worked as a bricklayer on its construction.

From Lincoln's Inn you can cross Kingsway to reach Great Queen Street and the **Old Curiosity Shop,** a great depository for literary trinkets and prints.

HYDE PARK and MAYFAIR

The **Ring Road** angles around the northern end of Hyde Park from the Serpentine to Marble Arch. Diarist John Evelyn, who complained that he had to pay a fee for driving his carriage through the park in 1657, mentioned the carriage races which went on here. Samuel Pepys, who was very proud of his stylish carriage, boasted of bringing his wife here to ride among the fashionable. The Ring was a promenade for displaying clothes and carriages by day and dueling by night. There are dueling scenes here in Thackeray's *Henry Esmond* and in Richard Brinsley Sheridan's plays. East of Ring Road near Marble Arch is the Speaker's Corner, which is liveliest on Sunday afternoons.

From Marble Arch, four blocks south along Park Lane, Upper Brook Street leads into **Grosvenor Square.** Here is a statue of F. D. Roosevelt as part of a memorial to the Four Freedoms, one of them the freedom of expression. To a house that stood here, Dr. Samuel Johnson came repeatedly, to wait long hours, to ask Lord Chesterfield's backing for his projected dictionary. Dickens' friend, novelist Edward Bulwer-Lytton, lived at No. 12; and William Beckford, author of the famous Gothic novel *Vathek,* lived at No. 22.

Berkeley Square, which can be reached by going through the southeast corner of Grosvenor Square down to Mount Street and then turning left, is the Gaunt Square which figures so prominently in Thackeray's *Vanity Fair.* Becky Sharp's house is on Curzon Street, which comes in at the southwest corner of the square. She lived at No. 22, and Disraeli kept No. 19 as his London house.

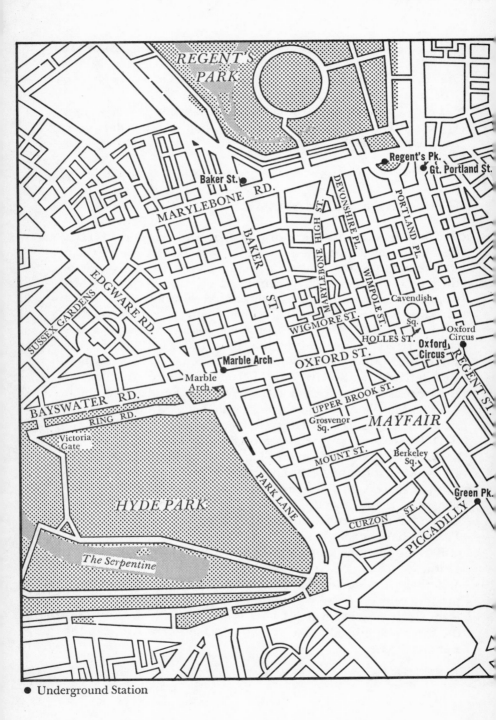

● Underground Station

SOUTH OF KENSINGTON GARDENS

Two blocks east of Kensington High Street Station is **Young Street,** where novelist William Makepeace Thackeray lived at No. 16 and wrote *Vanity Fair* and *Henry Esmond.* Two blocks north, on Kensington Palace Gardens, is **Kensington Palace,** once a royal residence but now a city museum. Many literary notables visited here in their time: novelist Horace Walpole; essayist, poet, and government official Joseph Addison; dramatist and government official William Congreve; and satirist and behind-the-scenes politician Jonathan Swift.

Back south on Palace Avenue and after turning east on Kensington Road along the gardens, you come to a little street called **Hyde Park Gate** on the south. Down this street, past a modern apartment development, sculptor Joseph Epstein made his home at No. 18. He cast the magnificent bronze busts of Joseph Conrad, Bernard Shaw, and W. B. Yeats, and the monument on Oscar Wilde's grave in Paris. At No. 22 writer Virginia Woolf was born. She lived here until her parents died and the four Stephen children took a house in Bloomsbury (see "British Museum Area").

The **Victoria and Albert Museum,** full of literary treasures, is only a few blocks away. The green dining room here was decorated by the artisan-writer William Morris and other members of the Pre-Raphaelite group. On display is a painting by Rossetti of his wife, with a poem dedicated to her right within the picture. Room 74 on the second floor, titled "The Art of the Book," has exhibits ranging from early illuminated manuscripts to present-day printing. Dickens' *A Tale of Two Cities* is one of many manuscripts here.

REGENTS PARK

One block west of Oxford Circus Underground is **Holles Street,** where Byron was born at No. 24 on January 22, 1788.

The Barretts' **Wimpole Street** is a few blocks to the north, and can be reached by going through the northwest corner of Cavendish Square to Wigmore Street, which leads directly into Wimpole on the right. At a house on the site of the present No. 50 the gifted poet Elizabeth Barrett lived with her tyrannical father, and it was from here that she eloped with Robert Browning. Farther up at No. 67 is the house from which Arthur Henry Hallam of Tennyson's *In Memoriam* left, never to return.

Wimpole Street then leads into **Devonshire Place**. At No. 2 Arthur Conan Doyle, a medical doctor as well as a weaver of mystery tales, had his office. Gothic novelist William Beckford lived at No. 4; and Monk Lewis, one of the earlier horror novelists, lived at No. 9.

Just north, at the intersection of **Marylebone Road** and **Marylebone High Street,** a few feet to the left as you come up from Devonshire Place, is a yellow office building which stands on the site of a house Charles Dickens lived in from 1839 to 1851. On the porch is a handsome bas-relief showing characters from some of the novels he wrote here—*The Old Curiosity Shop, Barnaby Rudge, Martin Chuzzlewit,* and *David Copperfield.* Next door is the St. Marylebone Parish Church, where the Brownings were secretly wed and the Dombeys of Dickens' *Dombey and Son* were married and their son, Paul, christened and buried.

Four blocks west is 221B **Baker Street,** the legendary address of Sherlock Holmes. From here sprang case after case in Arthur Conan Doyle's novels. The Marylebone Library a few yards away has an extensive collection of Sherlock Holmes material. In the Local History Room and the Archives Department on the first floor are copies of the *Baker Street Journal, Sherlock Holmes Journal,* books, biographies, posters, an enormous scrapbook of photographs, and a complete run of the *Strand Magazine* from 1915 to 1930.

ST. PAUL'S and NORTH

No church has as many monuments as **St. Paul's.** The Duke of Wellington is mounted on a horse thirty feet above the floor in the north choir aisle. Just in front of the aisle is a statue of Samuel Johnson, celebrated because the date of his death on its base is erroneous. The funeral took place on January 13, 1785, rather than on December 20, 1784. On the south side is a statue of John Donne, once dean of the cathedral. His was the only statue to survive the Great Fire of 1666.

In the crypt are the graves of George Cruikshank, the caricaturist who illustrated Dickens' books; Joshua Reynolds, famous portrait painter and close friend of Dr. Johnson, who also wrote on art and was an integral part of the eighteenth-century literary circle; poet Walter de la Mare and essayist Max Beerbohm, both of whom died in 1956.

At the end of the crypt is a tablet listing all of those notable persons who were buried in the old St. Paul's. Among them were Chaucer's friend and patron John of Gaunt, poets Philip Sidney and John Donne. In the adjoining St. Faith's Chapel is a memorial to William Blake with lines from his "Auguries of Innocence."

Almost near the end of the tomb of the Duke of Wellington are sculptures of Lawrence of Arabia and social novelist Charles Reade. Last is the famous Rodin bust of William Ernest Henley, inscribed with his famous lines, "I am the master of my fate, I am the captain of my soul."

St. Paul's and the street which encircles it were the hub of the early publishing industry. Printers first set up press in the courtyard during the early 1600's and stored their valuable manuscripts and books in the St. Faith's Chapel to protect them from the Great Fire. They were, unfortunately, completely destroyed along with the building, and it wasn't until 1710 that the publishers returned. Many of them survived until the Blitz during World War II.

Many first editions of Shakespeare were sold by publishers here. Near the cathedral's main entrance was the shop where

Dr. Johnson sold Goldsmith's novel, *The Vicar of Wakefield,* and thus saved the novelist from debtors' prison. The shop of J. Johnson was noted for publishing Cowper's long poem *The Task,* Blake's *The French Revolution,* and a number of Wordsworth's poems. Here Blake met the American revolutionist Tom Paine and social philosopher William Godwin. At one point a group of booksellers met here and decided to hire Dr. Johnson to write his great literary work, *Lives of the English Poets.* There are still a number of booksellers in the area, but their shops are all new, having been rebuilt after the war.

North of St. Paul's, over Newgate and through King Edward Street, is **Little Britain Street,** formerly Duck Lane, which during the eighteenth century was noted for printers and booksellers. Diarist Samuel Pepys records coming here to buy books and flirt with a bookseller's wife. England's first newspaper, the *Daily Courant,* was published here in 1702, as were the *Spectator* papers.

Little Britain Street leads north into Charterhouse Street and **Charterhouse Square** to the east. On the north side of the square are the Charterhouse buildings, in the seventeenth century a school for poor boys. Former students included essayist Joseph Addison, lyric poet Richard Lovelace, and William Makepeace Thackeray. It was also a place of refuge for old men. Thackeray's Colonel Newcome came here to school as a boy and returned to die an old man.

At the southwest corner of Charterhouse Square, **St. John Street** runs north from Charterhouse Street. Here is St. John's Gatehouse, erected in 1504, where Samuel Johnson worked when the building was the editorial and printing office of the *Gentlemen's Magazine.* His old pupil David Garrick is said to have given his first London performance before Johnson's working partners and friends. The gatehouse is all that is left of the old Priory of St. Johan, founded in about 1130 and suppressed by Elizabeth.

Going south again to the southwest corner of Charterhouse Square, Hayne Street leads to Long Lane and Kinghorn Street. This ancient narrow passage runs into **Bartholomew Close,** where John Milton, who had been very active in the Puritan government, hid in fear of vengeance for months during the

early part of the Restoration. This street winds back up into
Little Britain Street again.

SOHO

Piccadilly Circus is a good place to begin a tour of Soho.
From there you can head north over Sherwood Street, across
Brewer Street, and into **Golden Square.** The Viscount Bolingbroke, to whom Alexander Pope dedicated his *Essay on Man,*
lived about where No. 21 now stands. Jonathan Swift wrote of
dining with him here. Also, Matthew Bramble of Tobias Smollett's novel *Humphrey Clinker* lodged here with his entourage
while in London. Thackeray's Henry Esmond visited General
Webb at No. 22, and Ralph Nickleby of Dickens' *Nicholas
Nickleby* lived at No. 6.

On **Poland Street,** about six blocks north, Shelley lived at
No. 15 and from here took off with his neighbor Harriet West-
brook. William Blake lodged at No. 28 from 1785 to 1791, and
wrote his most famous works here. Up around the corner at
173 **Oxford Street** is the chemist's shop where Thomas De
Quincey, author of *Confessions of an English Opium-Eater,*
bought his first opium.

Soho Square lies about eight blocks east of the chemist's shop.
On the south side of this quaint little square, at 61 Greek
Street, is the house where the starving orphan Thomas De
Quincey landed one winter afternoon after wandering from
his boarding school in Wales, and became friendly with some
of the forlorn residents of this then seedy neighborhood. Becky
Sharp, of Thackeray's *Vanity Fair,* also lived here before her
marriage. On Frith Street, one block west, Hazlitt died at No. 6
and Mozart lived at No. 5.

Three blocks north from the meeting of Greek Street and
Shaftesbury Avenue is Dickens' Manette Street to the east.
Manette and Lucie, Darnay and Sydney Carton all lived here.
Just across Shaftesbury Avenue at Gerrard Street is the house
where Dryden lived and died, and the Turk's Head Tavern,

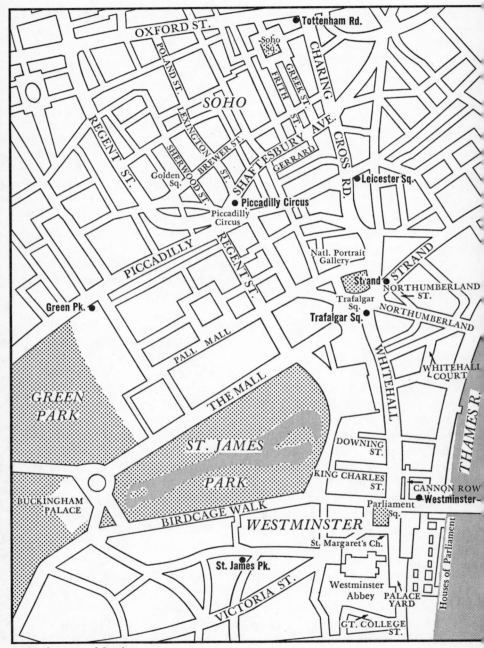

- Underground Station

where Joshua Reynolds and Samuel Johnson founded their famous club.

SOUTHWARK

Just south of London Bridge is **Southwark,** or St. Saviour's, Cathedral associated with several famous writers. The tower of this church was built by Chaucer's patron, John of Gaunt. Dramatists John Fletcher and Philip Massinger are buried here, along with Edmund Shakespeare, actor and brother of William, and Lawrence Fletcher, one of the co-owners of the Globe and Blackfriars theaters. A number of Elizabethan dramatists wrote and acted out their plays within the church. Shakespeare probably came here to watch his brother Edmund perform with the Southwark players. The Harvard Chapel was built as a memorial to Robert Harvard, founder of Harvard University, who was born above his father's Bankside butcher shop in 1607. There are memorial windows to Chaucer and Bunyan, who preached at a chapel near here, and to Goldsmith, who set up offices as a doctor in Bankside. The cathedral houses the well-preserved tomb of Shakespeare's friend, 14th-century poet John of Gaunt.

Across from the cathedral, St. Thomas Street leads to **Guy's Hospital,** where John Keats was a medical student in the early 1800's. Between here and the Borough Underground, on **Borough High Street,** all the old inns were located. On the corner of a little alley called White House Yard, the White Hart Inn of Shakespeare's *Henry IV* and Dickens' *Pickwick Papers* stood. Nearby is the seventeenth-century George Inn, featured in Dickens' *Little Dorrit.* Farther down on this same side is another little alley, **Talbot Yard;** the Old Tabard Inn on the corner there is on the approximate site of the Tabard Inn, from where the pilgrims of Chaucer's *The Canterbury Tales* left.

Just beyond Mermaid Court on the same side of the street was the **Old Marshalsea Prison,** where Thomas Malory, Ben Jonson, and John Donne were imprisoned for a while. In 1758 the prison was moved down about four blocks to Scovell Road.

It was at the new site that Charles Dickens' father was imprisoned as a debtor. At that time Dickens lodged in Lant Street, just a block south of the Borough Underground. That period in his life appears in several of his major novels. David Copperfield's father had been imprisoned as a debtor and David came to visit him often when he lived on **Lant Street.** He also visited the Micawbers, who were at King's Bench Prison just south of Lant Street. (Tobias Smollett was also confined there for a time for libeling an admiral.)

David Copperfield described his stay there: "a back attic was found for me at the house of an insolvent court agent who lived in Lant Street . . . a bed and bedding were sent over for me [from the Marshalsea] and made up on the floor. . . . The Crown Revenues are seldom collected in this happy valley; the rents are dubious, and the water is very frequently shut off." "There is," he continued, "an air of repose about Lant Street, which sheds a gentle melancholy on the soul . . . if a man wanted to abstract himself from the world . . . he should by all means go to Lant Street."

Marshalsea Road, west of Borough High Street, leads into the area where Shakespeare and his players performed. From Marshalsea, Southwark Bridge Road leads into **Park Street** on the west, going toward the river. About halfway down Park Street on the west side is a brewery with a polished gold plaque on the front, saying that the building is on the site of Shakespeare's Globe. However, current speculation suggests that the theater actually may have been closer to the river. During Shakespeare's time there was also a bearbaiting garden right across the street.

Dr. Samuel Johnson often came to Park Street to visit his friends the Thrales. Joshua Reynolds, Oliver Goldsmith, and David Garrick frequented the house also. Up on the river, about a block to the east on **Bankside,** is the Anchor Inn, visited by Johnson and his friends. Its precursor was a gathering place for Elizabethan theatergoers. **Clink Street** on the east was the site of Clink Prison, considered the lowliest place to be incarcerated in London. From its name comes the expression "in the clink." This street continues on back to Southwark Cathedral.

THE STRAND and TEMPLE AREAS

Several blocks east of Trafalgar Square on the river is **Charing Cross Station** and its network of railways. This station covers the Old Hungerford Stairs, where Dickens worked at Warren's Blacking Factory while his father was imprisoned as a debtor in Marshalsea Prison. The house he lived in here and the shoe-blacking factory are featured in *David Copperfield* as Murdstone and Grinby's "down in Blackfriars."

Just past Villiers Street, the first street to the east back up on the Strand, is **Buckingham Street,** where Samuel Pepys once lived at the existing No. 12. Across the way at No. 15 Charles Dickens lived briefly and had Betsey Trotwood take rooms for David Copperfield. Between 1609 and 1737 a huge shopping center called the New Exchange was built in this area alongside the Strand. Samuel Pepys wrote of shopping here, and many scenes from the plays of Dryden and Wycherley were laid in the shops.

No. 142 **Strand** was once the home of Chapman's Publishing Company, where literary persons sometimes lodged in the nineteenth century. Among them were American poet and essayist Ralph Waldo Emerson and novelist George Eliot (Mary Ann Evans), who met her lifelong companion, George Lewes, here. Chapman and Hall, the publishers who put out most of Dickens' novels, were at No. 186. Dickens was said to have come here to read aloud a copy of a short story which he had placed anonymously in *Old Monthly Magazine*. Thus began his long relationship with them.

Aldwych, the crescent forming an arc between the law courts and Wellington Streets, is the hub of the legitimate theater district. Right across the way on the Strand stands **Somerset House,** which registers documents having to do with births, deaths, and marriages. You can walk inside to look at the wills of Shakespeare, Milton, and Dr. Johnson. The building itself, built in the 1600's, housed the Royal Academy and Royal Society until the mid-nineteenth century, when they moved to Burlington House. On this site was once another Somerset House, a seventeenth-century royal palace where plays and masques by dramatists Francis Beaumont, Thomas Dekker, and Ben Jonson were often performed—complete with sets by Inigo Jones.

Across the Strand toward the Aldwych arc is the Church of **St. Mary-le-Strand,** the left of two islands. Though not Wren's, the steeple is considered one of the most noteworthy in London. A bit of trivia: Dickens' parents were married here. The neighboring island is occupied by **St. Clement Dane's Church,** where Dr. Johnson worshiped.

Across from the entrance to Middle Temple Lane here is the **Temple Bar,** straddling the Strand. This was the old gateway to the city of London, which went east from here. Almost on this spot Daniel Defoe was detained in a pillory for writing *The Shortest Way with the Dissenters,* a document ironically advocating the exile or execution of all Dissenters, including himself. As the story goes, London citizens realized how the authorities had been taken in by a joke and they decorated the pillory with flowers.

The drum-shaped **Round Temple Church** on the right, built in 1185 by the crusading Order of the Knights Templars in commemoration of the Temple Solomon in Jerusalem, has been romanticized since its completion during the reign of Henry II. If the church is open, you can see those cross-legged effigies of which Hazlitt once wrote. Oliver Goldsmith is buried here in the north side of the churchyard, just above the choir loft. And the tomb of another lesser-known writer, John Selden, a seventeenth-century historian and jurist, is located behind a slab of glass just to the left of the south-door entrance.

A little to the east of Temple Church is **St. Dunstan's-in-the-West,** an eighteenth-century structure restored in the 1830's and again after World War II. Among the list of vicars at the front entrance to the parish is poet John Donne, who served here between 1624 and 1631. There is also a small sculpture of Donne on the left of the church porch, and on the opposite side a corresponding facsimile of Charles Lamb, who supposedly wept when the church was being stripped of its embellishments to prepare for the restoration in 1831, for he feared that it would

ST. JOHN ST.

Charterhouse Sq.

ST. JOHN ST.

HAYNE ST.

LONG LANE

CHARTERHOUSE ST.

BARTHOLOMEW CLOSE

LITTLE BRITAIN

KING EDWARD ST.

ST.

NEWGATE ST.

St. Paul's

St. Paul's

NEW BRIDGE ST.

Blackfriars

Holborn Circus

HOLBORN

Chancery Lane

Took's Court

CURSITOR ST.

CHANCERY

THEOBALD'S RD.

LANE

FLEET ST.

Temple Ch.

MIDDLE TEMPLE

CROWN OFFICE ROW

HIGH HOLBORN

Old Sq.

New Sq.

LINCOLN'S INN FIELDS

Ch. of Mary-le-Strand

BRICK COURT

Fountain Court

LANE

Temple

VICTORIA EMBANKMENT

THAMES R.

KINGSWAY

GT. QUEEN ST.

ALDWYCH

Aldwych

Somerset House

Holborn

WELLINGTON ST.

STRAND

BUCKINGHAM ST.

VILLIERS ST.

NEW OXFORD ST.

CHARING CROSS RD.

Trafalgar Sq.

● Underground Station

not be rebuilt. Izaak Walton was an active member during the years he lived on Fleet Street. He was also Donne's biographer and often heard the great poet-preacher thunder out his magnificent sermons.

A success in the hosiery business, Walton served as "scavenger, quitsman, and sidesman" at St. Dunstan's. Then at age fifty he retired to his cottage at Shallowford (see entry) to engage in writing and angling, and wrote his world-renowned work *The Compleat Angler,* and a number of biographies, among them one of John Donne. Among several friends pictured with him in the church's stained-glass window are George Herbert, the poet. The grave of poet Thomas Campion, who so influenced Robert Herrick, was lost before the restoration.

Down Middle Temple Lane through Wren's gatehouse is Fountain Court and the entrance to **Middle Temple Hall,** where Shakespeare is said to have acted in the first performance of his own *Twelfth Night,* staged for Queen Elizabeth in 1602. Before going into the hall, note the fountain on the right side. In Dickens' *Martin Chuzzlewit,* which describes the area vividly, Ruth Punch waited here for her brother under the trees.

Beside the fountain commemorating Charles Lamb, who grew up here at the Inns of Courts, is a stone figure of a boy holding a book on which is inscribed a quotation from Lamb's essay on the temple, "Lawyers were children once."

Middle Temple had been a church until 1608, when the two Inns of Court, the Inner and Middle Temples, were established here. Among its famous members were such literary artists as novelists Henry Fielding and William M. Thackeray; politician Edmund Burke; poets Thomas More, Nicholas Rowe, and William Cowper; and dramatists William Congreve, Richard Brinsley Sheridan, and John Ford.

Inner Temple can be reached by an archway on the opposite side. Among its famous members have been dramatists William Wycherley and William Beaumont and the biographer Boswell. The south wall of the building holds a plaque by Charles Lamb: "Cheerful Crown Office Row (place of my kindly engenderence) a man would give something to have been born in such a place." Before leaving, take a look at the Raleigh coat of arms in one of the stained-glass windows.

Nearby, at 17 **Crown Office Row,** Charles Lamb lived as a boy, since his father was a servant to the bencher of the Inner Temple. It is said that he often wandered in and out of the gate leading to the Inner Temple. In 1775, a year before Charles was born at No. 2, Oliver Goldsmith died in the temple. Charles's older sister related the sorrows of his death as they walked around the court together. (The Lambs lived in this area until 1816, when they moved to Russell Street in Covent Garden.)

Goldsmith first lived in Garden Court, Middle Temple, where he wrote *The Traveller,* which came out in 1764, and later *The Vicar of Wakefield,* which made him a success. He also wrote *The Good Natur'd Man,* which David Garrick refused for the Drury Lane Theatre but which Goldsmith was able to produce at Covent Garden. As he became more successful, he moved to 2 **Brick Court,** decorated it lavishly, and threw wild parties, which disturbed William Blackstone, then working in the flat below on his *Commentaries.*

At Brick Court Goldsmith wrote most prolifically—*The Deserted Village, She Stoops to Conquer,* which was produced at Covent Garden in 1773, and all of his rather inconsequential potboilers. When he died many mourners flocked into the home to pay tribute. It is said that Edmund Burke burst into tears and Joshua Reynolds, living in Leicester Square, was indisposed for a few days.

TOWER HILL and NORTH

Many literary figures have been imprisoned in the **Tower of London,** among them Thomas Malory, who was put here for writing *Morte d'Arthur,* and Samuel Pepys, who was suspected of having communicated with the Stuart pretender to the throne.

Shakespeare accepted the legend that the tower, still a royal residence in his day, had been founded by Julius Caesar, since a sector of the Roman city wall ran across it from north to south. A large part of *Richard III* took place in and around the tower. In the White Tower, Richard sent the Bishop of Ely on an errand to get rid of him while he plotted the murder of the young princes with the Duke of Buckingham. The funeral services of *Henry V* took place in the chapel.

You can get a full view of the tower and its grounds by crossing over Tower Bridge to the opposite side of the river. Just over the bridge is Pickleherring Street, where John Fastolfe, a rich, testy old warrior, who had become a legend by the time Shakespeare incorporated him into *Henry IV*, died a century and a half before the playwright's time.

A few blocks northwest of the tower, after you go west on Tower Street and north on Seething Lane to the corner of Hart Street, is **St. Olave's Church.** This is about all of Pepys's London left in the area. He attended the church for about forty years and often wrote of his visits in the *Diary*.

The baroque gateway of St. Olave's is crowned by a formidable array of spikes, skulls, and crossbones carved in stone, all a reminder of the plague years. Pepys referred several times to the churchyard, which was much larger in his day. After the Great Plague of 1665 he wrote of how frightening it was to pass through it, as so many interments of plague victims had recently been made there. Dickens later referred to it as the churchyard of St. Ghastly Grim. One of the features that disappeared during the Blitz of World War II was the outside staircase which Pepys used to reach his seat in the Navy Pew. From his pew he could look directly across to ponder the memorial bust of his wife, which he had placed high up in the east end of the sanctuary. Pepys survived his wife by over thirty years, and the burial register at St. Olave's includes the following entry: "1703. Samuel Pepys, Esq. . . . buried in a vault under ye communion table." The coffin was found intact during the restoration of the church in 1954.

Just a few blocks north up Hart Street, which leads into Jewry Street, at the meeting of Fenchurch and **Aldgate High Street,** is a plaque on a post-office building saying that Geoffrey Chaucer lived there in 1374. At that time Aldgate, one of the medieval city gates, spanned the street on this site. Chaucer occupied one of the apartments above the gate.

TRAFALGAR SQUARE DOWN TO WESTMINSTER ABBEY

Hidden behind the National Gallery on Trafalgar Square is the **National Portrait Gallery,** which houses many fine portraits of writers, some done by artists closely associated with the authors in various groups and movements. Among the moderns are the famous Yeats portrait by Augustus John; D. H. Lawrence by Jan Junta, who worked with him on *Sea and Sardinia;* Dylan Thomas by Robert Sheppard; Sean O'Casey by Powys Evans; Vanessa Bell by Duncan Grant; Virginia Woolf by Francis Dodd; Leonard Woolf by Vanessa Bell; Bertrand Russell by Roger Fry, and another caricature of Russell done for *Punch* by Sir Bernard Partridge; the semi-abstract of T. S. Eliot by Patrick Heron; and many others.

Up in the Victorian section are the Brownings, Darwin, Tennyson, Matthew Arnold, Ruskin, Trollope, Dickens, Thackeray, Carlyle, De Quincey, Swinburne, George Eliot, and Charlotte Brontë. Nearby is the famous portrait of Jane Austen by her sister Cassandra, and the painting of the Brontë sisters by their brother, Branwell. In Room 17 are the Romantic poets, among them the meditating Wordsworth by Helvellyn and the only portrait of Shelley. Noble Lord Byron stands staunch and glamorous in his Albanian costume, which still survives and can be seen intact at the Museum of Costume in Bath.

Perhaps the most famous oil in the museum is that of Dr. Samuel Johnson by Joshua Reynolds. There are reproductions of this in many literary places throughout the country. Second might be the Chandos portrait of Shakespeare, possibly his only true likeness and the first portrait to be hung in the gallery. He is painted as a successful actor-manager of mature years, with keen, pentrating eyes and a gold earring. Not only portraits but photographs and films as well are included in this vast selection.

A few hundred yards off the square toward the river is the Sherlock Holmes Pub at 10 Northumberland Street, dedicated to preserving the legend of the great detective. Displayed in the

elaborately decorated Victorian bar on the lower floor is the
alleged head of the hound of the Baskervilles and the coiled
cobra described in "The Adventure of the Speckled Band."
Up a winding staircase on the second floor is a complete re-
construction of Sherlock Holmes's living room at the fictional
221B Baker Street. Everything is placed as if the master detective had just stepped out for a moment. A bust of Holmes,
in his deerstalker and cloak, presides over a realistic display of
almost every item mentioned in the stories or added by the
artists who depicted them—Holmes's violin and case, his curved
pipe, skeleton keys, magnifying glasses, masks, chemical ap-
paratus, even Watson's top hat, coat, and stethoscope. This display was assembled for the 1951 Festival of Britain. Just a few
blocks south toward Westminster is the real world of Scotland
Yard, which plays a part in countless mystery stories.

Back at Trafalgar Square, Whitehall leads down in the direction of Westminster Abbey. On the southeast just after you
leave the square is **Whitehall Court,** where H. G. Wells lived
for a while and where George Bernard Shaw kept a town residence. At the next corner is the famous **Banqueting Hall,** designed by Inigo Jones. In a previous hall on this site Shakespeare's *Othello* was first performed. In addition, many other
plays and masques by such dramatists as Jonson, Beaumont, and
Shirley were presented before royal audiences. This was at one
time a small part of Whitehall Palace, which spanned the distance from Great Scotland Yard to Big Ben, and in the other
direction from St. James's Park to the river. All but the Banqueting Hall burned to the ground in 1698. Sir Philip Sidney
and Sir Walter Raleigh often participated in tournaments
within the palace tiltyard, Milton worked within the palace, and
Samuel Pepys often came here on business. In the other halls of
the vast palace the courts of Queen Elizabeth I and Charles II
were also entertained by comedies, tragedies, and masques. On
King Street, which once ran through the palace grounds, poet
Edmund Spenser, author of *The Faerie Queene,* died in
poverty.

Just down from Banqueting Hall is **Downing Street,** where
Benjamin Disraeli and Winston Churchill lived at No. 10 during their tenures as Prime Minister. Just across the street Dr.

Johnson's biographer, James Boswell, wrote his slightly scandalous *London Journal,* and novelist Tobias Smollett had offices as a surgeon at a house nearby. Just off King Charles Street, the next street down, is **Cannon Row,** where Samuel Pepys often visited a wine house and wrote about pinching a barmaid there. John Locke was also living here while he wrote his *Essay Concerning Human Understanding.*

Across Parliament Square is the entrance to **Westminster Abbey.** In a former gatehouse that served as a prison in front of the entrance, Sir Walter Raleigh was imprisoned the night before his execution at the other end of the abbey. Samuel Pepys was incarcerated for corresponding with the exiled King James II, and Colley Cibber for getting into debt. The Jerusalem Chamber lies to the right of the main door before the entrance to the abbey. Shakespeare's Henry V was brought here after his fatal stroke, since it was predicted that he would die in Jerusalem. Later the chamber was a meeting place for literary men and scholars who gathered to compose the new King James version of the Bible.

Through the south aisle and straight ahead is the Poet's Corner, where most of the leading literary personalities of the abbey are buried. The wealth of talent crowded into this small area is quite awesome. Some, such as Chaucer, Browning, Tennyson, and T. S. Eliot, have elaborate memorials, while others are marked more simply by slabs on the floor. It is impossible to get around without treading on the remains of many writers.

Outside an arched entrance to the left of the main door is the Dean's Yard, so named since it was near the abbey's deanery. You can peek inside and see Ashburton House stretching across to the left. At one time the famous Cotton Library, now a part of the British Museum, was kept here.

Westminster School surrounds the Little Dean's Yard. Many celebrated writers attended here, among them William Cowper, Ben Jonson, John Locke, and Robert Southey. Next to the yard is Great College Street. To the right is Church House, covering the spot once occupied by No. 25, where John Keats lived before moving out to Hampstead to be with Fanny Brawne.

Beyond the Dean's Yard is Palace Yard. To the left the Henry VII Chapel of the abbey juts out. On this site was the cottage where Chaucer lived his last years and died. Chapter House is the octagonal spired building to the left of the chapel. On that site William Caxton set up England's first printing press and sold the country's first book.

To the right of Palace Yard stands Westminster Hall, which dates back to 1099. Both Thomas More and Richard Brinsley Sheridan were brought to trial here. For centuries most of London's law courts were held along the walls of this hall, and in addition booksellers, stationers, and sellers of odd goods had booths here.

St. Margaret's Church stands across the street. Winston Churchill, Samuel Pepys, and John Milton were married here, and in the churchyard are the graves of William Caxton and the second wife and child of John Milton. Ben Jonson spent his last years at a little cottage which stood between this church and the abbey. Inside are two windows donated by Americans. One in memory of John Milton has an inscription by the American poet John Greenleaf Whittier, and another in memory of Sir Walter Raleigh has an inscription by the American poet James Russell Lowell.

On the opposite side of the river, across from the Houses of Parliament, is **St. Thomas's Hospital,** where Somerset Maugham practiced medicine and set part of his novel *Of Human Bondage.*

Index